PAINTING & DECORATING

PAINTING &
DECORATING
JACKSON & DAY

HarperCollins*Publishers*

Published by HarperCollins Publishers
London

This book was created exclusively for
HarperCollins Publishers by
Jackson Day Jennings Ltd trading as
Inklink.

**Design, art direction
and project management**
Simon Jennings

Text
Albert Jackson
David Day

**Text and
editorial direction**
Albert Jackson

Illustrations editor
David Day

**Designer and
production assistant**
Alan Marshall

Illustrators
David Day
Robin Harris

Additional illustrations
Brian Craker
Michael Parr
Brian Sayers

First published in 1989
This edition published 1992,
reprinted in 1993

The text and illustrations in this book
were previously published in
Collins Complete DIY Manual

Copyright © 1986, 1989, 1992
HarperCollins Publishers

ISBN 0 00 412813 3

A catalogue record for this book is
available from the British Library

Printed and bound in Hong Kong

Picture credits
Albert Jackson: 6BR
almilmö Ltd: 16TR
B. C. Sanitan: 17BR
Berger Decorative Paints: 14TL, 15TR
Clive Helm: 13C, 14BL, 16BR, 17TR
Crown Decorative Products Ltd: 9BC
Faber Blinds (GB) Ltd: 7CR, 16BC
Frank Herholdt: 13T
Jerry Tubby: 16TR
Michael Dunne: 7BC, 17TL
Neil Lorimer: 10BR
Paul Chave: 8, 10T, 12, 31, 33, 36, 42, 44, 50, 51, 59, 60,
61
Rodney Hyett: 14BR, 17BC
Sheppard Day Designs: 13BR
Simon Jennings: 24, 26, 28, 30
Smallbone: 11BR, 13BL, 15TL
The Bisque Radiator Shop: 7TR
Tim Street-Porter: 9BR
Wrighton International Ltd: 10BL

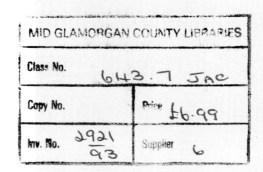

CONTENTS

Cross-references
There are few DIY projects that do not require a combination of skills. Decorating a single room, for instance, might also involve modifying the plumbing or electrical wiring, installing ventilation or insulation, repairing the structure of the building and so on. As a result, you might have to refer to more than one section of this book. To help you locate the relevant sections, a symbol (▷) in the text refers you to a list of cross-references in the page margin. Those references printed in bold type are directly related to the task in hand. Other references which will broaden your understanding of the subject are printed in light-weight type.

A BASIS FOR SELECTING COLOUR

Developing a sense of the 'right' colour is not the same as learning to paint a door or hang wallpaper. There are no 'rules' as such but there are simple guidelines which will help. In magazine articles on interior design or colour selection you will come across terms such as harmony and contrast. Colours are described as being cool or warm, or as tints or shades. These specialized terms form a basis for developing a colour scheme. By considering colours as the spokes of a wheel, you will see how one colour relates to another and how such relationships create a particular mood or effect.

Primary colours

All colours are derived from three basic 'pure' colours – red, blue and yellow. They are known as the primary colours.

Secondary colours

When you mix two primary colours in equal proportions, a secondary colour is produced. Red plus blue makes violet, blue with yellow makes green and red plus yellow makes orange. When a secondary colour is placed between its constituents on the wheel, it sits opposite its complementary colour – the one primary not used in its make-up. Complementary colours are the most contrasting colours in the spectrum and are used in colour schemes for dramatic effects.

Tertiary colours

When a primary is mixed equally with one of its neighbouring secondaries, it produces a tertiary colour. The complete wheel illustrates a simplified version of all colour groupings. Colours on opposite sides of the wheel are used in combination to produce vibrant, contrasting colour schemes, while those colours grouped together on one side of the wheel form the basis of a harmonious scheme.

Warm and cool colours

The wheel also groups colours with similar characteristics. On one side are the warm red and yellow combinations, colours we associate with fire and sunlight. A room decorated with warm colours feels cosy or exciting depending on the intensity of the colours used. Cool colours are grouped on the opposite side of the wheel. Blues and greens suggest vegetation, water and sky, and create a relaxed airy feeling when used together.

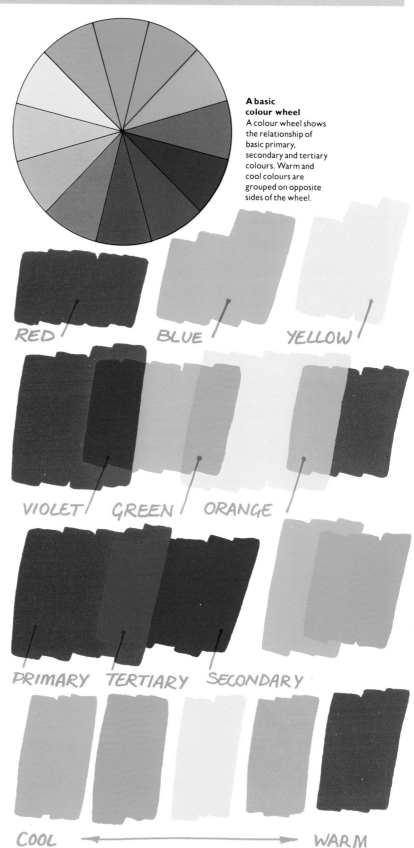

A basic colour wheel
A colour wheel shows the relationship of basic primary, secondary and tertiary colours. Warm and cool colours are grouped on opposite sides of the wheel.

RED

BLUE

YELLOW

VIOLET

GREEN

ORANGE

PRIMARY   TERTIARY   SECONDARY

COOL ⟵⟶ WARM

SELECTING COLOUR

1△

3▷

4▷

5▷

2▽

**1 Bold treatment
for a living room**
A bold red treatment
always creates a warm
atmosphere. In this
interior, obvious brush
strokes add the extra
element of texture.

2 A child's playroom
Primary colours make
a lively, invigorating
playroom. The grey
floor and expanse of
white accentuate the
bright colours.

**3 Coloured
equipment**
Basic appliances such as
baths, sinks or storage
heaters were
invariably produced in
neutral colours so that
they blended into any
interior. Now it is
possible to order
equipment like these
wall-mounted
radiators which
become important
elements of a colour
scheme.

**4 Adding colour
with window blinds**
Coloured or patterned
curtains are fairly
commonplace but
fewer people choose
from the available
range of brightly
coloured venetian
blinds. Strong sunlight
contributes to the
colourful effect.

**5 Using colour
outside**
Most buildings do not
lend themselves to
being painted in bright
colours. In areas of the
country where colour
is traditionally
acceptable, a bold
treatment can be very
exciting.

7

USING TONE FOR SUBTLETY

Pure colours are used to great effect for exterior colour schemes and interior decor but a more subtle combination of colours is called for in the majority of situations. Subtle colours are made by mixing different percentages of pure colour, or simply by changing the tone of a colour by adding a neutral.

Neutrals

The purest form of neutral is the complete absence of 'colour' – black or white. By mixing the two together, the range of neutrals is extended almost indefinitely as varying tones of grey. Neutrals are used extensively by decorators because they do not clash with any other colour, but in their simplest forms neutrals can be either stark or rather bland. Consequently, a touch of colour is normally added to a grey to give it a warm or cool bias so that it can pick up the character of another colour in harmony, or provide an almost imperceptible contrast within a range of colours.

Tints

Changing the tone of pure colours by adding white creates pastel colours or tints. Used in combination, tints are safe colours. It is difficult to produce anything but a harmonious scheme whatever colours you use together. The effect can be very different, however, if a pale tint is contrasted with dark tones to produce a dramatic result.

Shades

The shades of a colour are produced by adding black to it. Shades are rich dramatic colours which are used for bold yet sophisticated schemes. It is within this range of colours that browns appear – the interior designer's stock in trade. Brown blends so harmoniously into almost any colour scheme that it is tantamount to a neutral.

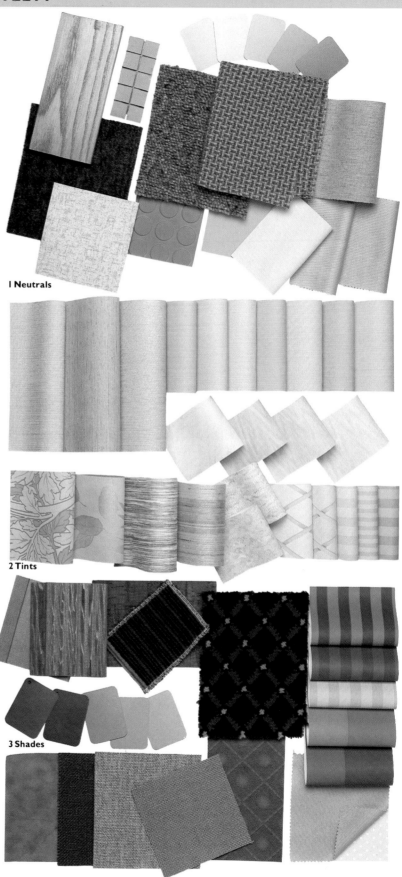

1 Neutrals

2 Tints

3 Shades

1 Neutrals
A range of neutral tones introduces all manner of subtle colours.

2 Tints
A composition of pale tints is always harmonious and attractive.

3 Shades
Use darker tones, or shades, for rich dramatic effects.

USING TONE

1△

◁2

3▷

1 White makes a room spacious
White paint, fabric and carpet take full advantage of available natural light to create a fresh airy interior. In this bedroom, the crisp black frames accentuate the beautifully proportioned windows.

2 Using tints creatively
Pale colours are often used when a safe harmonious scheme is required but you can create vibrant effects by juxtaposing cool and warm tints.

3 Dark dramatic tones
The very dark tone used for walls, ceiling and floors in this room is relieved by a carefully painted frieze and white accessories. Gloss paint will reflect some light even when such a dark colour is used.

9

TAKING TEXTURE INTO ACCOUNT

Colour is an abstraction, merely the way we perceive different wavelengths of light, and yet we are far more aware of the colour of a surface than its more tangible texture which we almost take for granted. Texture is a vital ingredient of any decorative scheme and merits careful thought.

Natural and man-made textures
(Far right)
Many people are not conscious of the actual texture of materials. This selection ranges from the warmth of wood and coarsely woven materials to the smooth coolness of marble, ceramics, plastic and metal.

Textural variety
(Below)
It's relatively simple to achieve interesting textural variety with almost any group of objects. Here, a few stylish kitchen artefacts contrast beautifully with a patterned tile splashback and warm oak cupboards.

The visual effect of texture is also created by light. A smooth surface reflects more light than one that is rough. Coarse textures absorb light, even creating shadows if the light falls at a shallow angle. Consequently, when you paint a coarse texture, the colour will look entirely different from the same colour applied to a smooth one.

Even without applied colour, texture adds interest to a scheme. You can contrast bare brickwork with smooth paintwork, for instance, or use the reflective qualities of glass, metal or glazed ceramics to produce some stunning decorative effects.

Just as colour is used to create an atmosphere, texture will produce an almost instinctive impression – it's as if we could feel texture with our eyes. Cork, wood, coarsely woven fabrics or rugs add warmth, even a sense of luxury, to an interior, while smooth hard materials such as polished stone, stainless steel, vinyl, or even a black lacquered surface, give a clean, almost clinical feeling to a room.

Carefully chosen textures *(Right)*
Soft and hard textures have been selected with care for this cool sophisticated environment.

USING PATTERN FOR EFFECT

Recent, purist approaches to design have made us afraid to use pattern boldly, and yet our less-inhibited forefathers felt free to cover their homes with pattern and applied decoration with spectacular results, creating a sense of gaiety, excitement – 'punch', if you like – which is difficult to evoke in any other way.

A well-designed patterned wallpaper, fabric or rug can provide the basis for the entire colour scheme and a professional designer will have chosen the colours to form a pleasing combination. There is no reason why the same colours shouldn't look equally attractive when applied to the other surfaces of a room but perhaps the safest way to incorporate a pattern is to use it on one surface only to contrast with plain colours elsewhere.

Combining different patterns can be tricky, but a small regular pattern normally works well with large, bold decoration. Also, different patterns with a similar dominating colour can coordinate well even if you experiment with contrasting tones. Another approach is to use the same pattern in different colourways, one for the walls perhaps and the other for curtains. You should also select patterns according to the atmosphere you want to create. Simple geometric shapes are likely to be more restful than bold swirling motifs.

Be bold with pattern
There is no reason to be afraid of using pattern when you consider that manufacturers have done most of the thinking for you. Well-designed materials are available to clad just about any surface in your home.

1 Coordinated pattern
The colours used for the striped curtain and furniture fabrics are the basis of this coordinated colour scheme.

2 A profusion of pattern
This bedroom combines a wealth of pattern with the rich colour of natural mahogany furniture. It shows what can be achieved if one has the courage to opt for the bold approach.

MANIPULATING SPACE

There are nearly always areas of a house that feel uncomfortably small or, conversely, so spacious that one feels isolated, almost vulnerable. Perhaps the first reaction is to consider structural alterations like knocking down a wall or installing a false ceiling. In some cases, such measures will prove to be the most effective solution, but there is no doubt that they will be more expensive and disruptive than the alternative measures of manipulating space – using colour, tone and pattern.

Our eyes perceive colours and tones in such a way that it is possible to create optical illusions that apparently change the dimensions of a room. Warm colours appear to advance, so that a room painted overall with brown or red, for instance, will feel smaller than the same room decorated in cool colours such as blue or green which have a tendency to recede.

Tone can be used to modify or reinforce the desired illusion. Dark tones, even when you are using cool colours, will advance, while pale tones will open up a space visually.

The same qualities of colour and tone will change the proportion of a space. Adjusting the height of a ceiling is an obvious example. If you paint a ceiling a darker tone than the walls it will appear lower. If you treated the floor in a similar way, you could almost squeeze the room between the two. A long narrow passageway will feel less claustrophobic if you push out the walls by decorating them with pale, cool colours which will, incidentally, reflect more light as well.

Using linear pattern is another way to alter our perception of space. A vertically striped wallpaper or woodstrip panelling on the walls counteracts the effect of a low ceiling. Venetian blinds make windows seem wider, and stripped wooden floors are stretched in the direction of the boards. Any large-scale pattern draws attention to itself and will advance like warm, dark colours, but small patterns appear as an overall texture from a distance so have less effect.

Practical experiments *(Right)*
A model will help to determine whether an optical illusion will have the desired effect.

Warm colours appear to advance

A cool colour or pale tone will recede

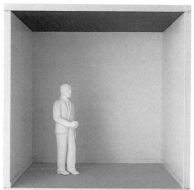

A dark ceiling will appear lower

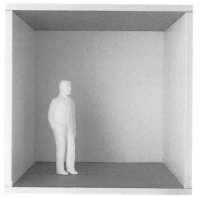

A dark floor and ceiling make a room smaller

Horizontal stripes make a wall seem wider

Vertical stripes increase the height

Large-scale patterns advance

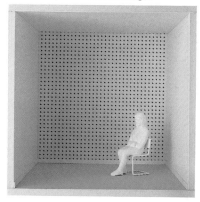

A small regular pattern recedes

1 Using mirrors
Floor to ceiling mirrors appear to double the size of a room.

2 Lowering a ceiling
A dark-tone carpet and deep-blue ceiling reduce the height of a room.

3 Incorporating an alcove
Disguise a small kitchen alcove by using colours or pattern which make it feel like part of the living room.

4 Creating space with pattern
A three-dimensional pattern can make a small space seem larger.

1△

2△

◁3

4▷

VERIFYING YOUR SCHEME

Before you spend money on paint, carpet or wallcoverings, collect samples of the materials you propose to use in order to gauge the effect of one colour or texture on another.

Collecting samples
Make your first selection from the limited choice of furniture fabrics or carpets. Collect offcuts of the other materials you are considering or borrow sample books or display samples from the suppliers to compare them at home. As paint charts are printed you can never be absolutely confident they will match the actual paint. Consequently, some manufacturers produce small sample pots of paint to try on the wall or woodwork.

Making a sample board
Professional designers make sample boards to check the relative proportions of materials as they will appear in the room. Usually a patch of floor- or wallcovering will be the largest dominating area of colour, painted woodwork will be proportionally smaller and accessories might be represented by small spots of colour. Make your own board by gluing your assembly of materials to stiff card, butting one piece against another to avoid leaving a white border around each sample which would change the combined effect.

Incorporating existing features
Most schemes will have to incorporate existing features such as a bathroom suite or kitchen units. Use these items as starting points, building the colour scheme around them. Cut a hole in your sample board to use as a window for viewing existing materials or borrowed examples against those on the card.

Checking your colour selection
View your completed sample board in natural and artificial light to check your colour selection.

SCHEMES FOR LIVING ROOMS

In most homes the living room is the largest area in the house. It's where you spend most of your leisure time and entertain your friends. It's the room upon which most money is spent on furnishings, curtains and carpets, not to mention expensive hi-fi units, the television set and so on. For all these reasons, you will want to make sure that the living room decor has lasting appeal. After all, you are unlikely to replace costly furniture and materials frequently.

Unless you are lucky enough to have more than one reception or living room, it is an area that must feel comfortable during the day, relaxing in the evening and lively enough for the occasional party. Unless the room receives an unusual amount of sunlight, a warm colour scheme is often the best, to create a cosy atmosphere. Dark cool tones will produce a similar result under artificial light, but very deep tones can have the opposite effect by creating dark shadowy areas. Predominantly neutral schemes or a range of browns and beiges lend themselves to change in the future by simply swapping the

accessories without having to spend a lot of money on replacing the essentials. Natural textures are equally versatile.

Patterned carpets or rugs are less likely to be ruined by the inevitable spillages than plain colours, but very dark tones are almost as difficult to keep clean as pale colours.

Curtains or blinds provide the perfect solution to a change of mood. During the day, they are pulled aside or withdrawn and therefore contribute very little to the general appearance of the room, but in the evening they can become a wall of colour or pattern which can transform the scheme.

An adaptable scheme
(Right)
A safe yet comfortable scheme lends itself to change by swapping the accessories.

Typically traditional
(Far right)
Pink-washed walls and floral patterns suit a typical country cottage.

Sympathetic style
(Below)
A surviving period living room deserves appropriate styling.

Simple styling suits a modern house *(Right)*
A modern home can be treated successfully with restrained colours and natural textures.

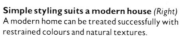

SCHEMES FOR BEDROOMS

A bedroom is first and foremost a personal room. Its decor should reflect the character of its occupant and the functions to which the room is put. At night, a bedroom should be relaxing, even romantic. Much depends on the lighting, but pattern and colour can create a luxurious and seductive mood.

Strangely, very few people ever use pattern on a ceiling, and yet a bedroom provides the ideal opportunity, especially as you are unlikely to spend much of your waking life there so can afford to be adventurous with the decor. Bedroom carpet is invariably of inferior quality because it need not be hardwearing but you could give the colour scheme a real lift by investing in an expensive rug or deep-pile carpet knowing that it will come to no harm.

If a bedroom faces south, early sunlight will provide the necessary stimulus to wake you up, but a north-facing room will benefit from bright invigorating colours.

Some bedrooms may serve a dual function. A teenager's bedroom may have to double as a study or a private sitting room so needs to be stimulating rather than restful. A child's room will almost certainly function as a playroom. The obvious choice would be for strong, even primary colours, but as most children accumulate brightly coloured toys, books and pictures you might select a neutral background to the colourful accessories. The smallest bedrooms are usually reserved for guests, but they can be made to appear larger and more inviting by the judicious manipulation of the proportions with colour or tone.

◁1

2▷

◁3

4▷

1 An elegant master bedroom
The peaceful character of this elegant bedroom is a result of a basically neutral scheme which is warmed very slightly by a hint of cream and pale yellow.

2 Bright and refreshing
The combination of bright yellow and white makes for a cheerful start to the day.

3 Dual-purpose room
When a bedroom doubles as a sitting room it needs to be stimulating during the day and cosy at night.

4 A guest room
A guest room should make a visitor feel at home immediately. The warmth of stripped pine makes this room very inviting.

DECOR FOR COOKING AND EATING

Kitchens need to be functional areas capable of taking a great deal of wear and tear, so the materials you choose will be dictated largely by practicalities. But that doesn't mean you have to restrict your use of colour in any way. Kitchen sinks and appliances are made in bright colours as well as the standard stainless steel and white enamel. Tiled worktops and splashbacks, vinyl floorcoverings and melamine surfaces offer further opportunity to introduce a range of colours.

Textures are an important consideration with a range of possibilities. Natural timber is still a popular material for kitchen cupboards, and wherever wood is employed, it will provide a warm element which you can choose to contrast with cool colours and textures, or pick up the warm theme with paint, paper or floor-covering. Some people prefer to rely entirely on metallic, ceramic and plastic surfaces which impose a clean, purposeful and practical character.

If the kitchen incorporates a dining area, you may decide to create within the same room a separate space that is more conducive to relaxation and conversation. Softer textures such as carpet tiles, cork flooring and fabric upholstery absorb some of the sound generated by appliances and the clatter of kitchen utensils. You could also decorate the walls in a different way to change the mood, perhaps using darker tones or a patterned wallcovering to define the dining area.

1 A functional kitchen
This simple kitchen, laid out to form a perfect work triangle, looks extremely functional without feeling clinical.

2 A family kitchen
Some people like the kitchen to be part of an informal sitting and dining area where the family can relax.

3 A breakfast room
A sunny alcove linked to the kitchen makes an ideal breakfast room.

4 A kitchen extension
Colourful fabric blinds shade this kitchen extension from direct sunlight.

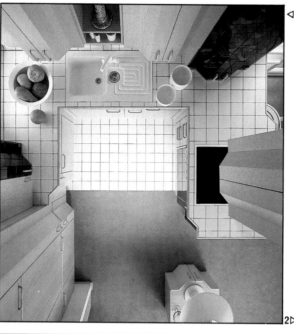

BATHROOMS

Bathrooms like kitchens must fulfil quite definite functions efficiently but they should never look clinical. Even when a bathroom is centrally heated, a cold uninviting colour scheme would not be a wise choice as enamelled and tiled surfaces are inevitable. Coloured bathroom appliances are commonplace but choose carefully as they are likely to remain the dominating influence on any future colour schemes.

A bathroom is another area where you can afford to be inventive with your use of colour or pattern. A bold treatment which might become tiresome with overexposure can be highly successful in a room used at intervals only. Try to introduce some sound-absorbing materials like ceiling tiles, carpet or cork flooring to avoid the hollow acoustics associated with old-fashioned tiled bathrooms. If you want to use delicate materials that might be affected by steam, make sure the bathroom is

properly ventilated. Bathrooms are usually small rooms with relatively high ceilings, but painting a ceiling a dark tone which might improve the proportion of a larger room can make a bathroom feel like a box. A more successful way to counter the effect of a high ceiling is to divide the walls with a dado rail, using a different colour or material above and below the line.

If you live in a hard-water area, avoid dark-coloured bathroom suites which will emphasize lime-scale deposits.

1 Warm and luxurious
There is no reason why a bathroom cannot be warm and inviting when there is such a choice of luxurious wallcoverings and ceramic tiles.

2 Changing the proportion
Improve the proportion of a bathroom with a high ceiling by a change of colour at dado height.

3 Fashionable styling
A clever combination of colour and shape changes a simple bathroom into a room with distinctive character.

4 A period bathroom
Reproduction fittings and marbled paintwork re-create a period bathroom.

Ladder accessories
Kit out your ladder with a range of helpful devices to make working easier and safer. This ladder features adjustable feet (1) for uneven ground, a foot rest for comfort (2), a clamp for a paint can (3), a tool tray (4), and a stay (5), to hold the top away from eaves or gutters.

BEFORE YOU BEGIN

Timing, weather and the condition of the site are important factors to consider before you decorate outside. Indoors, you have the problem of what to do with a room full of furniture and furnishings while you work.

OUTSIDE THE HOUSE

Plan your work so that you can begin the actual decoration of the house exterior in late summer and autumn so that the previous warm weather will have dried out the fabric of the building sufficiently.

The best weather for decorating is a warm but overcast day. Avoid painting on rainy days or in direct sunlight, as both can ruin new paintwork. You should follow the sun around the house, however, so that its warmth dries out the night's dew before you get there.

Don't work on windy days either, or dust will be deposited on the fresh paint. Sprinkle water around doorways or spray with a houseplant spray before you paint as this settles dust, which you would churn up with your feet.

Clear away any rubbish from around the house, which will slow down your progress or even cause accidents. Cut back overhanging foliage from trees or shrubs. Protect plants and paving with dust sheets in the work area.

INSIDE THE HOUSE

Before you decorate a room inside, carry out all repairs necessary and have the chimney swept if you use an open fire: a soot fall would ruin your decorations. Clear as much furniture from the room as possible, and group what is left under dust sheets.

Lift any rugs or carpets then spray water on the floor and sweep it to collect loose dust before you begin to paint. Protect finished wood or tiled floors with dust sheets.

Remove all furnishings such as pictures and lampshades and unscrew door handles and fingerplates. Keep the knob handy in the room with you, in case you get shut in accidentally.

WHAT TO WEAR

Naturally, you will wear old clothes when decorating, but avoid woollen garments, which tend to leave hairs sticking to paintwork. Dungarees with loops and large pockets for tools are ideal for decorating and other work.

MEANS OF ACCESS

Whether you are decorating inside or outside, you must provide adequate means of reaching the area you are working on. Using inefficient equipment and makeshift structures is dangerous; but even if you don't want to buy your own ladders, you can hire them quite cheaply. Safety and comfort while working are other important considerations, and there's a range of devices and accessories to make the job that much easier.

Types of ladders and access equipment

Stepladders are essential for interior decoration. Traditional wooden stepladders are still available, but they have been largely superseded by lightweight aluminium alloy types. You should have at least one pair which stand about 2m (6ft 6in) high to reach a ceiling, without having to stand on the top step. Another, shorter ladder might be more convenient for other jobs and you can use them both, with scaffold boards, to build a platform.

Outdoors you'll need ladders to reach up to eaves height. Double and triple wooden extension ladders are very heavy, so consider a metal one.

Some doubles and most triples are operated by a rope and pulley so that they can be extended single-handed.

To estimate the length of ladder you need, add together the ceiling heights of your house. Add at least one metre (about 3ft) to the length to allow for the angle and access to a platform.

There are many versions of dual- or even multi-purpose ladders, which convert from stepladder to straight ladder. A well-designed, versatile ladder is a good compromise.

Sectional scaffold frames can be built up to form towers at any convenient height for decorating inside and outside. Wide feet prevent the tower sinking into the ground, and adjustable versions allow you to level it. Some models have locking castors, which enable you to move the tower.

Towers are ideal for painting a large expanse of wall outdoors. Indoors, smaller platforms made from the same scaffold components bring high ceilings within easy reach.

Accessories for ladders

- **Ladder stay** A stay holds the ladder away from the wall. It is an essential piece of equipment when painting overhanging eaves and gutters: you would otherwise be forced to lean back and possibly overbalance.
- **Clip-on platform** A wide flat board, which clamps to the rungs, provides a comfortable platform to stand on while working for long periods.
- **Adjustable legs** Bolt-on accessories, which enable you to level the foot of a ladder on uneven ground.

- **Paint can holder** You should always support yourself with one hand on a ladder, so use a metal S-hook to hang the paint can from a rung. A special clamp, which can be fixed to the stile, enables you to position the can at one side of the ladder.
- **Tool tray** A clip-on tray is ideal for holding a small selection of tools.

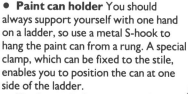

Alloy stepladder   **Dual-purpose ladder**   **Scaffold tower**   **Extending ladder**

WORKING WITH LADDERS

When you buy or hire a ladder, wooden or metal, bear in mind that:

● Wooden ladders should be made from straight-grained, knot-free timber.
● Good-quality wooden ladders have hardwood rungs tenoned through the upright stiles and secured with wedges.
● Wooden rungs with reinforcing metal rods stretched under them are safer than ones without.
● End caps or foot pads are an advantage to prevent the ladder from slipping on hard ground.
● Adjustability is a prime consideration. Choose a ladder that enables you to gain access to various parts of the building and which converts to a compact unit for storage.
● The rungs of overlapping sections of an extension ladder should align or the gap between the rungs might be too small to secure a good foothold.
● Choose an extension ladder with a rope, pulley and an automatic latch, which locks the extension to its rung.
● Check that you can buy or hire a range of accessories (see opposite) to fit your make of ladder.
● Choose a stepladder with a platform at the top to take cans and trays.
● Treads should be comfortable to stand on. Stepladders with wide, flat treads are the best choice.
● Stepladders with extended stiles give you a handhold at the top of the steps.
● Wooden stepladders often have a rope to stop the two halves sliding apart. A better solution used on most metal stepladders is a folding stay, which locks in the open position.

Is the ladder safe to use?

Check ladders regularly and before you use them after a winter's break. Inspect a hired ladder before use.

Look for splits opening along the stiles, check that there are no missing or broken rungs and that the joints are tight. Sight along the stiles to make sure they are aligned, or the ladder could rock when leant against a wall.

Inspect wooden ladders for signs of woodworm or rot. Even a few holes or sponginess could signify serious damage below the surface. Test that the wood is sound before using the ladder and treat it with a woodworm fluid or preservative. If in doubt, scrap the ladder for safety's sake.

Check that fixings for hinges and pulleys are secure and lubricate them. Inspect the pulley rope for fraying and renew if necessary.

Oil or varnish wooden ladders regularly to stop them drying out. Apply extra coats to the rungs (which take most wear). Don't paint a ladder as this may hide serious defects.

How to handle a ladder

Ladders are heavy and unwieldy; handle them properly so you don't damage property or injure yourself.

Carry a ladder upright, not slung across your shoulder. Hold the ladder vertically, bend your knees slightly then rock the ladder back against your shoulder. Grip one rung lower down while you support the ladder at head height with your other hand, then straighten your knees.

To erect a ladder, lay it on the ground with its feet against the wall. Gradually raise it to vertical as you walk towards the wall. Pull the feet out from the wall so that the ladder is resting at an angle of about 70 degrees – if the ladder extends to 8m (26ft) for example, its feet should be 2m (6ft 6in), or one quarter of its height, from the wall.

Raise an extending ladder to the required height while holding it upright. If it is a heavy ladder, get someone to hold it while you operate the pulley.

Handling a ladder
Carry the ladder upright, leaning back against your shoulder; grip one rung low down, another at head height. When erected, the base of the ladder should be one quarter of its height away from the wall so that it is correctly balanced.

HOW TO USE A LADDER SAFELY

More accidents are caused by using ladders unwisely than as a result of faulty equipment. Erect the ladder safely before you ascend and move it when the work is out of reach – never lean out to the side or you'll overbalance. Follow these simple, common-sense rules:

Securing the ladder
If the ground is soft, spread the load of the ladder by placing a wide board under the feet; screw a batten across the board to wedge the ladder in place.

On hard ground, make sure the ladder has anti-slip end caps and lay a sandbag (or a tough polythene bag filled with earth) at the base.

Secure the stiles near the base with rope tied to timber stakes driven into the ground at each side and just behind the ladder (**1**). When extending a ladder, the sections should overlap by at least one quarter of their length – but don't lean the top against the gutters, soil pipes and drainpipes, and especially glass, as they may give way.

Anchor the ladder near the top by tying it to a stout timber rail, held across the inside of the window frame. Make sure the rail extends about 300mm (1ft) on each side of the window and pad the ends to protect the wall (**2**).

It's a good idea to fix ring bolts at regular intervals into the masonry just below the fascia board: this is an excellent way to secure the top of a ladder as you have equally good anchor points wherever you position it. Alternatively, fix screw eyes to the masonry or a sound fascia board and attach the ladder to them.

Safety aloft
Never climb higher than four rungs from the top of the ladder or you will not be able to balance properly, and handholds will be out of reach. Don't lean sideways from a ladder either. Keep both feet on a rung and your hips centred between the stiles.

Avoid a slippery foothold by placing a sack or old doormat at the foot of the ladder to dry your boots and wipe off any mud before you ascend.

Unless the manufacturer states otherwise, do not use a ladder to form a horizontal walkway, even with a scaffold board lying on it.

Stepladders are prone to topple sideways. Clamp a strut to the ladder on uneven floors (**3**).

1 Staking a ladder
Secure the base of the ladder by lashing it to stakes in the ground.

2 Securing the top
Anchor the ladder to a batten held inside the window frame.

3 Supporting a stepladder
Clamp a strut to the stile to prop up a pair of stepladders.

ERECTING WORK PLATFORMS INDOORS

A lot of work can be carried out by moving a ladder little by little as the work progresses, but it can become tedious, perhaps leading to an accident as you try to reach just a bit further before having to move along, and then overbalance.

It's more convenient to build a work platform which allows you to tackle a large area without moving the structure. You can hire decorators' trestles and bridge a pair with a scaffold board, or make a similar structure with two pairs of stepladders (1).

Clamp or tie the board to the rungs and use two boards, one on top of the other, if two people need to use the platform at once.

An even better arrangement is to use scaffold tower components to make a mobile platform (2). Choose one with locking castors for the ideal solution for painting or papering ceilings.

2 Mobile platform
An efficient structure made from scaffold tower frames.

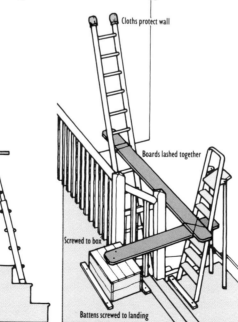

1 Improvised platform
A simple yet safe platform made from stepladders and a scaffold board.

Gaining access to a stairwell

Stairwells present particular problems when building work platforms. The simplest method is to use a dual-purpose staircase ladder, which can be adjusted to stand evenly on a flight (3). Anchor the steps with rope through a couple of screw eyes fixed to the stair treads; the holes will be concealed by carpet later. Rest a scaffold board between the ladder and the landing to form a bridge. Screw the board to the landing and tie the other end.

Alternatively, construct a tailor-made platform from ladders and boards to suit your staircase (4). Make sure the boards and ladders are clamped or lashed together, and that ladders can't slip on the treads. If necessary, screw wooden battens to the stairs to prevent the foot of the ladder moving.

Stair scaffold
Erect a platform to compensate for the slope of a staircase with scaffold frames.

3 Dual-purpose ladder
Use a stair ladder to straddle the flight with a scaffold board to give a level work platform.

Cloths protect wall

Boards lashed together

Screwed to box

Battens screwed to landing

4 Tailor-made platform
Build a network of scaffold boards, stepladders, ladders and boxes to suit your stairwell layout.

ERECTING PLATFORMS OUTSIDE

Scaffolding is by far the best method of building a work platform to decorate the outside of a house. Towers made from slot-together frames are available for hire. Heights up to about 9m (30ft) are possible; the tallest ones require supporting 'outriggers'.

Build the lower section of the frame first and level it with adjustable feet before erecting a tower on top. As you build, climb and stand on the inside of the tower.

Erect a proper platform at the top with toe boards all round to prevent tools and materials being knocked off the tower, and extend the framework to provide hand rails all round.

Secure the tower to the house by tying it to ring bolts fixed into the masonry, as with ladders.

Some towers incorporate a staircase inside the scaffold frame; floors with a trapdoor enable you to ascend to the top of the tower. If you cannot find such a tower, the safest access is via a ladder. Make sure it extends at least 1m (about 3ft) above the staging so that you can step on and off safely.

It is difficult to reach windows and walls above an extension with just a ladder. With a scaffold tower, however, you can construct a cantilevered section fixed to the main tower, which rests on the roof of the extension.

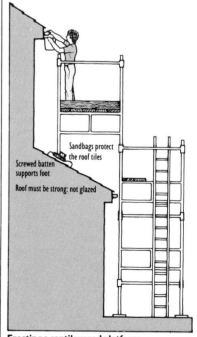

Sandbags protect the roof tiles

Screwed batten supports foot

Roof must be strong: not glazed

Erecting a cantilevered platform
The cantilever section rests on a board to spread load.

PREPARATION AND PRIMING

Thorough preparation of all surfaces is the vital first step in redecorating. If you neglect this stage, subsequent finishes will be rejected. Preparation means removing dirt, grease and loose or flaky previous finishes, as well as repairing serious deterioration such as cracks, holes, corrosion and decay. It's not just old surfaces that need attention: new masonry, timber and metalwork must be sealed against attack and priming is called for to ensure a surface is in a suitable condition to accept its finish. Consult the charts on this page for details of primers and sealers for all the materials you're likely to encounter in and around the home, then read the following sections, which examine each material in detail.

TYPES OF PRIMERS AND SEALERS

There are numerous primers and sealers to suit a variety of materials.

Stabilizing primer
Used to bind powdery or flaky materials. A clear or white liquid.

Wood primer
Standard pink or white primer prevents other coats of paint soaking in.

Aluminium wood primer
Used to seal oily hardwoods, it will also cover creosote.

General-purpose primer
Seals porous building materials and covers patchy walls and ceilings.

Metal primers
Essential to prevent corrosion in metals and to provide a key for paint.

PVA bonding agent
A general-purpose liquid adhesive for many building materials. An excellent primer and sealer when diluted, even for bituminous paints.

Water repellent
A liquid which dries colourless to seal masonry against water penetration.

Alkali-resistant primer
Used to prevent the alkali content of some materials attacking oil paints.

Aluminium spirit-based sealer
Formulated to obliterate materials likely to 'bleed' through subsequent coatings. Effective over bituminous paints, creosote, metallic paints and nicotine.

SEE ALSO

Details for: ▷	
Priming plaster	22
Priming wood	27
Priming metal	30

PRIMERS AND SEALERS   SUITABILITY: DRYING TIME: COVERAGE

● Black dot denotes that primer and surface are compatible.

● Red dot denotes metal primers.

SUITABLE FOR	Stabilizing primer	Wood primer	Aluminium wood primer	General-purpose primer	Zinc phosphate	Red oxide	Calcium plumbate	Red lead	Chromate primer	PVA bonding agent	Water repellent	Alkali-resistant primer	Aluminium sealer spirit-based
Brick	●			●						●	●	●	
Stone	●			●						●	●	●	
Cement rendering	●			●						●	●	●	
Concrete	●			●						●	●	●	
Plaster	●			●						●		●	
Plasterboard	●			●								●	
Distemper	●												
Limewash	●												
Cement paint	●												
Bituminous paints										●			●
Asbestos cement	●			●						●		●	
Softwood		●	●	●				●					
Hardwood			●				●	●					
Chipboard		●	●	●				●					
Hardboard		●	●	●				●					
Plywood		●	●	●				●					
Creosoted timber			●										●
Absorbent fibre boards	●											●	
Ferrous metals (inside)					●	●							
Ferrous metals (outside)					●		●						
Galvanized metal							●						
Aluminium					●				●				

DRYING TIME: HOURS													
Touch dry	3	6	6	4	4	4	8	10	10	3	1	4	1/4
Recoatable	16	16	16	16	10	16	24	24	24	16	12	16	1

COVERAGE (Sq. metre per litre)													
Smooth surface	9	13	15	12	13	13	13	13	13	9	3-4	10	4
Rough/Absorbent surface	7	10	11	9	10	10	10	10	10	7	2-3	7	3

● **Lead content in paint**
Lead, which is a poison, was widely used in the past as a drier in solvent-based paints including primers. (Emulsions, which are water-based, have never contained lead). Many solvent-based paints are now made without lead. If possible, choose one labelled 'no lead added' or similar. Don't let children chew old painted surfaces, which may have a high lead content.

PLASTERWORK: MAKING GOOD

Plaster is used to finish the inner surfaces of the walls and ceilings in most houses. Ceilings are traditionally clad with slim wood laths which are then plastered over: the plaster grips between the laths. Walls are usually covered directly with a backing (floating) coat of plaster and a smooth finish coat – various grades of plaster are used to suit the condition and quality of the masonry.

In very old houses, the walls might be lath-and-plaster covered. In modern houses, plasterboard is used instead for convenience. A plastered or boarded surface can be decorated with paint, paper or cladding such as tiles; the preparation is similar for each. Whatever you intend to use as a decorative finish, the plastered wall or ceiling must be made good by filling cracks or holes.

Cracks in solid plaster

Rake loose material from a crack with the blade of a scraper or filling knife (**1**). Undercut the edges of larger cracks to provide a key for the filling. Mix up interior-grade cellulose filler to a stiff consistency or use a pre-mixed filler.

Dampen the crack with a paintbrush, then press the filler in with a filling knife. Drag the blade across the crack to force the filler in then draw it along the crack (**2**) to smooth the filler. Leave the filler standing slightly proud of the surface ready for rubbing down smooth and flush with abrasive paper.

Fill shallow cracks with one application, but for deep ones, build up the filler in stages, letting each set before adding more.

Cracks sometimes appear in the corner between walls or a wall and ceiling; fill these by running your finger dipped in filler along the crack. When the filler has hardened, rub it down with medium-grade abrasive paper.

Fill and rub down small holes and dents in solid plasterwork in the same way as for filling cracks.

PREPARING TO DECORATE

NEW PLASTER

New plaster must dry out thoroughly before it can be decorated with paint or paper. Allow efflorescence to form on the surface then wipe off with coarse sacking; repeat periodically until the crystals cease to appear.

Use an alkali-resistant primer if you are applying oil paint. Priming isn't necessary for emulsion, but apply a thinned coat on absorbent plaster.

Size new, absorbent plaster before wallpapering, or the water will be sucked too quickly from the paste, resulting in poor adhesion. Use a proprietary size or heavy-duty wallpaper paste. If you are hanging vinyl wallcovering, make sure the size contains fungicide as the covering can't breathe like a plain paper can.

For tiling, no further preparation is needed, once the plaster is dry.

Smooth finish
Smooth the surface of small repairs with a wet brush or knife to reduce the amount of sanding required later.

OLD PLASTER

Apart from filling minor defects and dusting down, old dry plaster needs no further preparation. If the wall is patchy, apply a general purpose primer. If the surface is friable apply a stabilizing solution before you decorate.

Don't decorate damp plaster; cure, then let the plaster dry out first.

PLASTERBOARD

Fill all joints between newly fixed plasterboard then, whether you are painting or papering the board, daub all nail heads with zinc phosphate primer.

Before you paint plasterboard with oil paint, prime it with one coat of general-purpose primer. One coat of thinned emulsion may be needed on an absorbent board before the normal full-strength coats are applied.

Prior to hanging wallcovering on plasterboard, seal the surface with a general-purpose primer thinned with white spirit. After 48 hours, apply a coat of size. This allows wet-stripping without disturbing the board's paper facing.

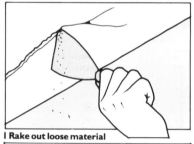

1 Rake out loose material

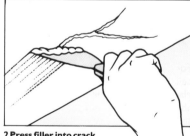

2 Press filler into crack

PAINTED PLASTER

Wash any paintwork in good condition with sugar soap or detergent solution to remove dirt and grease. Use water and medium-grade wet and dry abrasive paper to key the surface of gloss paint, particularly if covering with emulsion. Prime and allow to dry.

If the ceiling is severely stained by smoke and nicotine, prime it with an alkali-resistant primer or an aluminium spirit-based sealer.

If you want to hang wallcovering on oil paint, key then size the wall. Add dry plaster or cellulose filler to the size to provide an additional key. Cross-line the wall with lining paper (◁) before hanging a heavy embossed paper on oil paint.

Remove flaky materials with a scraper or stiff-bristled brush. Feather off the edges of the paintwork with wet and dry abrasive paper. Treat bare plaster patches with a general-purpose-primer. Should the edges of old paintwork continue to show, prime those areas again, rubbing down afterwards. Apply stabilizing primer if the paint is friable.

Apply tiles over sound paintwork after you have removed any loose material.

PATCHING HOLES IN PLASTER

A lath-and-plaster wall

If the laths are intact, plaster up the holes as for solid plasterwork. A hole under 75mm (3in) wide can simply be packed out with a ball of wet newspaper dipped in plaster. Fill flush to the surface with cellulose filler.

If some laths are broken, reinforce the repair with a piece of fine expanded metal mesh. Rake out loose plaster and undercut the edge of the hole with a bolster chisel. Use tinsnips to cut the

metal to the shape of the hole but a little larger (1).

The mesh is flexible so you can bend it in order to tuck the edge behind the sound plaster all round (2). Flatten it against the laths with light taps from a hammer and if possible staple the mesh to a wall stud to hold it (3).

Gently apply one thin coat of backing plaster (4) and let it dry for about one hour before you continue patching.

I Cut with tinsnips **2 Tuck mesh into hole** **3 Staple mesh to stud** **4 Trowel on plaster**

A plasterboard wall or ceiling

A large hole punched through a plasterboard wall or ceiling cannot be patched with wet plaster only. Cut back the damaged board to the nearest studs or joists at each side using a sharp trimming knife against a straightedge. Keep the cut-out slim to avoid having to fit braces at the long sides (1).

Cut a new panel of plasterboard to fit

snugly within the hole and nail it to the joists or studs using galvanized plasterboard nails. Use a steel trowel to spread finish plaster over the panel, forcing it well into the edges (2). Allow the plaster to stiffen then smooth over it with a dry trowel. You may have to add another layer to bring the patch to the level of the wall or ceiling.

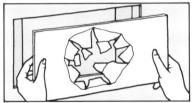 

I Cut damaged panel to nearest supports **2 Nail on the new panel and coat with plaster**

A small hole in plasterboard

For very small holes in plasterboard use cellulose filler instead of plaster. Use a glass-fibre patching tape for holes up to about 90mm (3½in) across. Stick on the self-adhesive strips in a star shape over the hole then apply filler (1).

Alternatively, use an offcut of plasterboard just larger than the hole yet narrow enough to slot through. Bore a hole in the middle and thread a

length of string through. Tie a galvanized nail to one end of the string (2). Butter the ends of the offcut with filler then feed it into the hole (3). Pull on the string to force it against the back of the cladding then press more filler into the hole so it's not quite flush with the surface. When the filler is hard, cut off the string then apply a thin coat of filler for a flush finish.

I Fill and feather the patch **2 Fix string to offcut** **3 Pull on string**

DEALING WITH DISTEMPER

Distemper was once a popular finish, so you may have to deal with it if your house is old. Distemper is basically powdered chalk or whiting, mixed with glue size and water. It makes a poor base for decorating: when wet it redissolves and comes away from the surface along with the new decorations.

To remove it, brush away all loose material and wash off what you can. A little wallpaper stripper in the water will help. Apply a stabilizing primer to bind any traces left on the surface.

Many delicate plaster mouldings have been obliterated over the years with successive coats of distemper. Being water-soluble, you can remove it with a lot of care and patience. Work on a small area at a time, wetting it through with water. Remove the distemper with an old toothbrush until the detail of the moulding becomes clear, then scrape out the softened paint with pointed sticks such as wooden skewers. Wash over the moulding finally and apply a stabilizing primer.

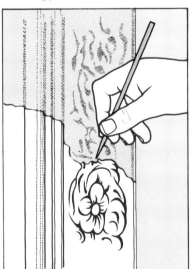

How to remove distemper
Scrub with a toothbrush, then scrape out the softened paint with a pointed stick.

Limewash and cement paints

Other water-thinned paints such as limewash and cement paints are less likely to cause problems when they're overpainted, unless they are in poor condition. Scrape and brush down with a stiff-bristled brush, then wipe the surface with white spirit to remove grease (it is best not to use water on these paints). Ensure the surface is sound by applying a stabilizing primer.

SEE ALSO

Details for: ▷
Primers   21

External corners
Dampen the chipped corner then use a filling knife to scrape the filler onto the damaged edge, working from both sides of the angle (1). Let the filler stiffen then shape it with a wet finger to closely resemble the original profile (2).

I Use filler knife

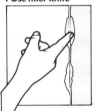

2 Shape with finger

● **Lath-and-plaster ceiling**
If the laths are sound, plaster over as for solid plasterwork. If the laths are broken, cut back to the nearest joist and secure with galvanized nails. Fit a panel of plasterboard and spread on a coat of bonding plaster followed by a coat of finish plaster.

ERADICATING MOULD GROWTH

When provided with damp conditions, mould can develop, usually in the form of black specks. The cause of the damp should be remedied before you treat the walls or ceiling.

Sterilize the mould growth before you carry out any other preparatory work to avoid distributing spores into the atmosphere. Apply a liberal wash of a solution made from 1 part household bleach: 16 parts water. Don't make the solution any stronger as it may damage the wall decoration. Leave the solution for at least four hours then carefully scrape off the mould, wipe it onto newspaper and burn it outside.

Wash the wall again with the solution but leave it for three days to sterilize the wall completely. When the wall is dry, paint it with a stabilizing primer thinned with white spirit. If you plan to hang wallpaper, size the wall using a size containing a fungicide solution.

Where mould growth is affecting wallpaper, soak the area in a warm water and bleach solution, then scrape off the contaminated paper and burn it. Wash the wall with a fresh bleach solution to remove paste residue.

Apply a liberal wash of similar solution to sterilize the wall and leave it for at least three days, but preferably one week, to make sure no further growth occurs. When the wall is completely dry, apply a stabilizing primer thinned with white spirit, followed by a coat of size if you plan to re-paper the wall.

2 Steam stripper
To remove painted and washable wallpapers, use a steam stripper – little more than a water boiler which exudes steam from a sole plate. To use the machine, hold the plate against the wall until the steam penetrates, soaks and softens the paper, then remove it with a scraper. Wash the wall to remove traces of paste.

Mould growth ▷
Mould, typified by black specks, will grow on damp plaster or paper.

PREPARING WALLCOVERINGS

Faced with a previously papered surface the best solution is to strip it completely before hanging new wallcoverings. However, if the paper is perfectly sound, you can paint it with emulsion or oil paints (but be warned: it will be difficult to remove in the future). Don't paint vinyl wallcovering except blown vinyl (◁). If the paper has strong reds, greens or blues, the colours may show through the finished paint; metallic inks have a similar tendency. You can mask strong colours by applying knotting thinned by 25 per cent with methylated spirit, but over a large area, use an aluminium spirit-based sealer. If you opt for stripping off the old covering, the method you use depends on the material and how it's been treated.

Stripping wallpaper

Soak the paper with warm water with a little washing-up liquid or proprietary stripping powder or liquid added to soften the adhesive. Apply the liquid with a sponge or houseplant sprayer. Repeat and leave the water to penetrate for 15 to 20 minutes.

Use a wide metal-bladed scraper to lift the softened paper, starting at the seams. Take care not to dig the points of the blade into the plaster. Re-soak stubborn areas of paper and return to strip them later.

Electricity and water are a lethal combination: where possible, dry-strip around switches and sockets. If the paper cannot be stripped dry, switch off the power at the consumer unit (◁) when you come to strip around electrical fittings. Unscrew the faceplates so that you can get at the paper trapped behind. Don't use the sprayer near electrical accessories.

Collect all the stripped paper in plastic sacks, then wash the wall with warm water containing a little detergent. From then on, treat the wall as for plaster (◁).

Scoring washable wallpaper

Washable wallpaper has an impervious plastic surface film, which you must break through to allow the water to penetrate to the adhesive.

Use a wire brush, coarse abrasive paper or a serrated scraper to score the surface, then soak it with warm water and stripper. It may take several applications of the liquid before the paper begins to lift.

Peeling off vinyl wallcovering

Vinyl wallcovering consists of a thin vinyl layer, which is fused with the pattern, on a paper backing. It is possible to peel off the film, leaving the backing paper on the wall; this can then be painted or used as a lining for a new wallcovering.

To remove the top layer, lift both bottom corners, then pull firmly but steadily away from the wall. Either soak and scrape off the backing paper or, if you want to leave it as a lining paper, smooth the seams with medium-grade abrasive paper, but use very light pressure or you'll wear a hole.

Stripping painted wallcoverings

Wallcoverings which have been painted previously can be difficult to remove, especially if a heavy embossed paper was used. If the paper is sound, prepare in the same way as painted plaster (◁) and decorate over it.

Use a wire brush or home-made scraper (**1**) to score the surface then soak with warm water plus a little paper stripper. Painted papers (and washables) can easily be stripped using a hired steam stripper. Hold the stripper plate against the paper until the steam penetrates, then remove the soaked paper with a wide-bladed scraper (**2**).

1 Wallpaper scorer
Drive some nails through a block of softwood measuring about 150mm x 125mm x 25mm (6in x 5in x 1in), so that the points just protrude.

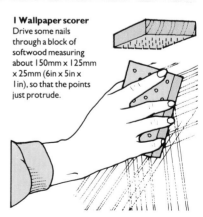

SANDING A WOODEN FLOOR

A sanded wooden floor sealed with a clear finish that highlights its grain is a most attractive feature for many rooms. Although straightforward, the job is laborious, dusty and extremely noisy. Considerable patience is also required in order to achieve an even, scratch-free and long-lasting finish.

Repairing the floorboards

There's no point in spending time and money sanding floorboards which are in poor condition, so examine them first. Look for any boards with signs of woodworm infestation. If the beetle is still active, treat the remaining boards and joists below with a proprietary woodworm fluid. Even if the beetle has been eradicated, replace any boards with more than a few holes in them: beneath the surface there may be a honeycomb of tunnels made by the woodworm larvae. As the sanding process will remove a lot of timber, these tunnels may be revealed on the surface of the boards.

If you find signs of dry or wet rot when you lift a floorboard, have it treated straightaway before you continue with the sanding.

Examine the floor for boards which have been lifted previously by electricians and plumbers. Replace any that are split, too short or badly jointed Try to find secondhand boards to match the rest of the floor, but if you have to use new wood, stain it after the floor is sanded to match the colour of the old boards. Drive all nail heads below the surface with a punch and hammer: a raised head will rip the abrasive paper on the sander's drum.

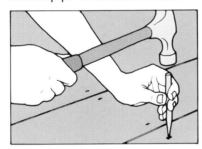

Sink nail heads below the surface

Filling gaps between floorboards

What you do about gaps between boards depends on how much they bother you. Many people simply ignore them, but you will end up with a superior job as well as improved draughtproofing if you make the effort to fill them invisibly or close them up.

Closing up
Over a large area, the quickest and most satisfactory solution is to lift the boards a few at a time and re-lay them butted side by side, filling in the final gap with a new board.

Filling with papier mâché
If there are a few gaps only, make up a stiff papier mâché paste with white newsprint and wallpaper paste, plus a little water-based wood dye to colour it to match the sanded floor. Scrape out dirt and wax from between the boards and press the paste into the gap with a filling knife. Press it well below the level likely to be reached by the sander, and fill flush with the floor surface. Run the blade along the gap to smooth it.

Inserting a wooden lath
Large gaps can be filled by a thin wood lath planed to fit tightly between the boards. Apply a little PVA adhesive to the gap and tap the lath in with a hammer until it is flush with the surface. Skim it with a plane if necessary. Don't bother to fill several gaps this way: it is easier to close up the boards and fill one gap only with a new floorboard.

Force papier mâché between boards

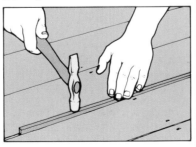

Wedge a wooden lath into a wide gap

CHOOSING A SANDING MACHINE

The area of a floor is far too large to contemplate sanding with anything but an industrial sanding machine. You can obtain such equipment from the usual tool hire outlets, which also supply the abrasive papers. You will need three grades of paper: coarse, to level the boards initially, medium and fine to achieve a smooth finish.

It's best to hire a large upright drum sander for the main floor area and a smaller rotary sander for tackling the edges. For small rooms such as bathrooms and WCs, you can use the rotary sander only.

Some companies also supply a scraper for cleaning out the inaccessible corners, but do make sure it is fitted with a new blade when you hire.

SEE ALSO

Details for: ▷
Wood stains   42

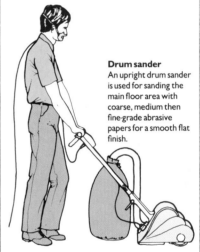

Drum sander
An upright drum sander is used for sanding the main floor area with coarse, medium then fine-grade abrasive papers for a smooth flat finish.

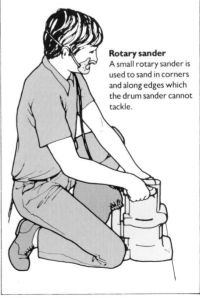

Rotary sander
A small rotary sander is used to sand in corners and along edges which the drum sander cannot tackle.

Hook scraper
Use a small hook scraper for removing paint spots from the floor, and for reaching into spaces that are inaccessible to the rotary sander. The tool cuts on the backward stroke; various sizes and blade shapes are available to deal with most situations.

25

USING SANDING MACHINES

Fitting the abrasive sheet

Precise instructions for fitting the abrasive paper to the sanding machine should be included with the hire kit, or the hirer will demonstrate what you need to do. Never attempt to change abrasive papers while the machine is plugged into a socket.

With most machines the paper is wrapped round the drum and secured with a screw-down bar (1). Ensure that the paper is wrapped tightly around the drum: if it is slack it may slip from its clamp and will be torn to pieces.

Edging sanders take a disc of abrasive, usually clamped to the sole plate by a central nut (2).

I Drum sander   2 Rotary sander

Operating a drum sander

Stand at the beginning of a run with the drum sander tilted back so that the drum itself is clear of the floor. Drape the electric lead over one shoulder to make sure it cannot become caught in the sander.

Switch on the machine then gently lower the drum onto the floor. To hold the machine still for even a short time will sand a deep hollow in the floor. There is no need to push a drum sander: it will move forward under its own power. Hold the machine in check so that it proceeds at a slow but steady walking pace along a straight line.

When you reach the other side of the room, tilt the machine back, switch off and wait for it to stop before lowering it to the floor.

If the paper rips, tilt the machine onto its back castors and switch off. Wait for the drum to stop revolving, disconnect the power then change the paper: if you let go of the machine it will run across the room on its own, almost certainly damaging the floor in the process.

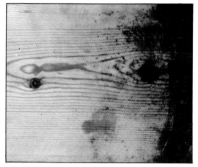

Sanding cleans and rejuvenates wooden floors

Using an edging sander

Hold the handles on top of the machine and drape the flex over your shoulder. Tilt the sander onto its back castors to lift the disc off the floor. Switch on and lower the machine. As soon as you contact the boards, sweep the machine in any direction but keep it moving. As soon as it comes to rest the disc will score deep, scorched swirl marks in the wood, which are difficult to remove. There is no need to press down on the machine. When you have finished, tilt back the machine and switch off, leaving the motor to run down.

I Sand diagonally across the floorboards

Sanding procedure

A great deal of dust is produced by sanding a floor, so before you begin, empty the room of furniture and take down curtains, lampshades and pictures. Seal around the room door with masking tape and stuff folded newspaper under it. Open all windows. Wear old clothes and a gauze facemask.

Sweep the floor to remove grit and other debris. Old floorboards will most likely be curved across their width, or cupped, so the first task is to level the floor across its entire area.

With coarse paper fitted in the drum sander, sand diagonally across the room (1). At the end of the run, tilt the machine, pull it back and make a second run parallel to the first. Allow each pass to slightly overlap the last.

When you have covered the floor once, sand it again in the same way, but this time across the opposite diagonal of the room (2). Sweep the sawdust from the floor after each run is completed.

Once the floor is flat, so that the boards are clean all over, change to a medium grade paper and sand parallel to the boards (3). Overlap each pass as before. Finally, switch to the fine grade paper to remove all obvious scratches and give a smooth finish.

Sand the edges of the room with the rotary machine. As soon as you change the grade of paper on the drum sander, put the same grade on the edging sander. In this way, the edges of the room are finished to the same standard as the main area (4).

Even the edging sander cannot clean right up to the skirting or into the corners; finish these small areas with a scraper, or fit a flexible abrasive disc in a power drill.

Vacuum the floor and wipe it over with a cloth dampened with white spirit ready for finishing.

2 Sand across the opposite diagonal

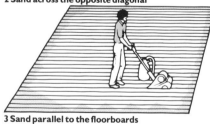

3 Sand parallel to the floorboards

4 Finish the edges with the rotary sander

The wooden joinery in our homes needs redecorating long before any other part of the house, particularly on the exterior of windows and doors, bargeboards and fascias. The cause is the nature of the wood itself, which swells when it becomes moist, then shrinks again when the sun or central heating dries it out. Paint will not adhere for long under these conditions, nor will any other finish. Wood is also vulnerable to woodworm and various forms of rot caused primarily by damp, so it is not surprising that careful preparation is essential to preserve most types of timber.

Treating new timber

A lot of new joinery is primed at the factory but check that the primer is in good condition before it is installed: there may have been a long delay before it was delivered. Don't leave it uncovered outside, either, as primer itself is not sufficient protection against prolonged exposure to the weather. If the primer seems to be satisfactory, rub it down lightly with fine-grade abrasive paper, dust it off, then apply a second coat of wood primer to the areas that will be inaccessible after installation.

To prepare bare timber, first make sure it is dry, then sand the surface in the direction of the grain only, using a fine-grade glasspaper (wrap it round a wood block for flat surfaces; roll it round a pencil or piece of dowel for moulded sections).

Once you have removed all raised grain and lightly rounded sharp edges, dust the wood down. Rub it over finally with a tack rag – an impregnated cloth to which dust will stick; they're sold in many DIY stores.

Seal resinous knots with shellac knotting

Knots and other resinous areas of the wood must be treated to prevent them staining subsequent paint layers. Pick off any hardened resin, then seal the knots by painting them with two coats of shellac knotting. This is the best material to use when you plan to paint with pale finishing colours; for darker paints, seal the knots and prime the timber in one operation using aluminium primer.

Alternatively, paint bare timber with a standard resin-based primer or use a quick-drying water-thinned acrylic primer. Apply either liberally, taking care to work it well into the joints and particularly the end grain (which will require at least two coats to give it adequate protection).

Wash oily hardwoods with white spirit immediately prior to priming with an aluminium primer. For other hardwoods, use oil- or water-thinned wood primers, thinned slightly to encourage penetration into the grain.

When the primer is dry, fill open-grained timber with a fine surface filler. Use a piece of coarse cloth to rub it well into the wood. Use circular strokes followed by parallel strokes in the direction of the grain. When the filler is dry, rub it down with a fine abrasive paper to a smooth finish.

Fill larger holes, open joints, cracks and similar imperfections with interior or exterior wood filler. Press it into holes with a filling knife, leaving it slightly proud of the surface so that it can be sanded flush with fine-grade abrasive paper once it has set. Dust down ready for painting. If you find a hole you have missed just before you start applying the undercoat, fill it with putty; unlike other fillers, you can paint straight over putty without having to wait for it to dry, although you should wait until it forms a skin.

Filling the grain

If you plan to clear-finish an open-grained timber, apply a proprietary grain filler after sanding. Use a natural filler for pale timbers: for darker wood, buy a filler that matches the timber. Rub the filler across the grain with a coarse rag, leave to harden for several hours, then rub off the excess along the grain with a clean coarse rag.

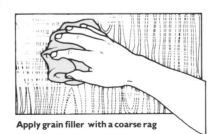
Apply grain filler with a coarse rag

Preparing for a clear finish

There's no need to apply knotting when you intend to finish the timber with a clear varnish or lacquer. Sand the wood in the direction of the grain using progressively finer grades of abrasive paper, then seal it with a slightly thinned coat of the intended finish.

If the wood is in contact with the ground or in proximity to previous outbreaks of dry rot, treat it first with a liberal wash of clear timber preservative. Check with the maker's recommendations that the liquid is compatible with the finish. This treatment is equally well suited to a painted finish.

Cellulose filler would show through a clear finish, so use a proprietary stopper to fill imperfections: these are thick pastes made in a range of colours to suit the type of timber. You can adjust the colour further by mixing it with wood stains. As stoppers can be oil- or water-based, make sure you use a similarly-based stain. Where possible, use an oil-based stopper outside. Fill the blemishes as before and rub down when the stopper hardens.

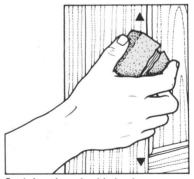
Sand along the grain with abrasive paper

PAINTED AND VARNISHED WOODWORK

Most of the joinery in and around your house will have been painted or varnished at some time and so long as it is in good condition, it will form a sound base for new paintwork. But when too many coats of paint have been applied, mouldings around door and window frames begin to look poorly defined and the paintwork has an unattractive, lumpy appearance; it's best to strip off all the old paint to bare wood and start again. Stripping off is also essential where the paintwork has deteriorated and is blistering, crazing or flaking.

Liquid sander
You can chemically prepare paintwork in good condition using a liquid sander: wipe it onto the surface with a cloth or sponge and leave it to slightly soften the top layer of paint, leaving a matt finish. It is an ideal surface for applying the new top coat of paint. The chemical cleans and degreases the paintwork, too.

Dry, flaky paintwork

Heavily overpainted woodwork

Preparing paintwork in good condition

Wash the paintwork from the bottom upwards with a solution of warm water and sugar soap or detergent. Pay particular attention to the areas around door handles and window catches, where dirt and grease will be heaviest. Rinse with fresh water from top to bottom to prevent runs of dirty liquid on a newly cleaned surface.

Use fine grade wet and dry abrasive paper dipped in water to rub down gloss paintwork, providing a key for the new finish coat, and remove any blemishes. Prime bare patches of wood. Build up these low spots gradually with undercoat, rubbing down between each application.

Fill any open joints or holes with filler and rub down when set. Renew old and crumbling window putty and seal around window and door frames with mastic (◁). Proceed with your chosen undercoat and top coat, following the basic paint system (◁).

Preparing unsound paintwork or varnish

Unsound paintwork or varnish such as the examples pictured left must be stripped to bare wood. There are several methods you can use but always scrape off loose material first.

In some cases, where the paint is particularly dry and flaky, dry-scraping may be all that is required, using a proprietary hook scraper (◁), plus a light rub down with abrasive paper. Where most of the paint is stuck firmly to the woodwork, remove it using one of the methods described below and on the facing page.

Stripping paint and varnish with a blowtorch

The traditional method for stripping old paint is to burn it off with a flame. The paraffin-fuelled blowlamp has now been largely superseded by the more convenient, safer blowtorch, which is fuelled by liquid gas in a replaceable pressurized canister.

More sophisticated tools are designed so that the torch itself is connected by a hose to a metal gas bottle, the type used for camping or in caravans. This type of gas torch is finely adjustable, so is useful for other jobs such as brazing and soldering.

To reduce the risk of fire, take down curtains and pelmets and, outside, rake out old bird's nests from behind your roof fascia board and soffit.

It's only necessary to soften the paint with a flame, but it is all too easy to heat the paint so that it is actually burning when you scrape it off. Deposit these scrapings in a paint kettle or metal bucket as you remove them.

Start by stripping mouldings from the bottom upwards. Never direct the flame at one spot but keep it moving all the time, so that you do not scorch the wood. As soon as the paint has softened, use a shavehook to scrape it off easily. If it is sticky or hard, heat it a little more then try scraping again.

Having dealt with the mouldings, strip flat areas of woodwork, using a wide-bladed stripping knife. When you have finished stripping, sand the wood with medium-grade abrasive paper to remove hardened specks of paint and any accidental light scorching.

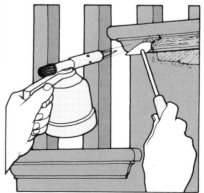
Shavehook, used for mouldings

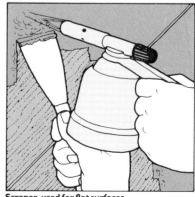
Scraper, used for flat surfaces

Badly weathered varnish

SELECTING AND USING CHEMICAL STRIPPERS

An old finish can be removed using a stripper which reacts chemically with paint or varnish. There are basically two types: those with a liquid or gel consistency based on methylene chloride; and strippers in the form of a thick paste, which are caustic based.

All chemical strippers can be dangerous if splashed on your skin or eyes, so take proper precautions:
● Wear vinyl work gloves and safety spectacles. If you have a respiratory problem, wear a face mask, too.
● Work in a well-ventilated area and never smoke near the chemicals: some give off fumes which are toxic when inhaled through a cigarette.
● If you get stripper on your skin, wash it off immediately with copious amounts of cold water. If it gets in your eyes, wash it out under running water and seek medical advice.
● Keep pets and small children out of the way when using chemical strippers.

GEL OR LIQUID STRIPPERS

Liquid strippers are only suitable when you can lay an object horizontal. For stripping household joinery, use a gel stripper, which is stiff enough to cling to vertical surfaces.

Lay polythene sheet or plenty of newspaper on the floor, then apply a liberal coat of stripper to the paint, working well into the mouldings.

Leave it for about 10 minutes then try scraping a patch to see if the paint has softened through to the wood. If not, don't waste time removing the top layers only, but apply more stripper and stipple the softened paint back down with a brush. Leave for five minutes.

Once the chemicals have completed their work, use a stripping knife to scrape the paint from flat surfaces and a shavehook to remove it from mouldings.

Wipe the paint from deep carvings with fine wire wool; use small pieces of coarse sacking when stripping oak as particles of metal can stain the wood.

When you have removed the bulk of the paint, clean off residual patches with a wad of wire wool dipped in fresh stripper. Rub with the grain, turning the wad inside out to present a clean face as it becomes clogged with paint.

Neutralize the stripper by washing the wood with white spirit or water (depending on the manufacturer's advice). It is cheaper to use water when washing large areas but it will raise the grain and can cause joints to swell. Let the wood dry out thoroughly then treat as new timber (▷).

PASTE STRIPPERS

Spread a paste stripper onto wood in a thick layer, working it well into crevices and mouldings and making sure all air bubbles are expelled.

The paste must be kept moist long enough for the chemicals to work – it may dry out too quickly in direct sunlight or a heated room – so cover it with a thin polythene sheet. Some manufacturers supply a blanket which seals the moisture in. Leave the stripper in place for several hours, then lift the leathery substance at the edge with a scraper and peel it off, complete with paint, in one layer. If it has become too hard to peel, soften it by soaking.

Discard the paste wrapped in newspaper, then wash the wood with water and a scrubbing brush. Leave it to dry before priming and finishing.

INDUSTRIAL STRIPPING

Any portable woodwork can be taken to a professional stripper, who will immerse the whole thing in a tank of stripping solution. Many companies use a solution of hot caustic soda, which must be washed out of the wood by hosing down with water. It is an efficient process (which incidentally kills woodworm at the same time) but there is a risk of splitting the panels, warping the wood and of opening up joints. At best, you can expect a reasonable amount of raised grain, which you will have to sand before refinishing.

Some companies use a cold chemical dip, which does little harm to solid timber and raises the grain less. This process is likely to be more expensive than the caustic soda method.

Most stripping companies will collect, many will rehang a door for you, and some offer a finishing service, too.

Never submit veneered items to either treatment: it may peel off.

Using a hot air stripper

Although stripping paint with a flame is fast and efficient, there is always the risk that you will burn the wood. Scorching can be covered by paint, but if you want to varnish the stripped wood, scorch marks will mar the finish.

Electrically-heated guns – like powerful hair dryers – work almost as quickly as a torch with less risk of scorching or fire. They do operate at an extremely high temperature: under no circumstances test the stripper by holding your hand over the nozzle.

Some guns come with variable heat settings and a selection of nozzles for various uses (see below). Hold the gun about 50mm (2in) from the surface of the paintwork and move it slowly backwards and forwards until the paint blisters and bubbles. Immediately remove the paint with a shavehook or scraper. Aim to heat the paint just ahead of the scraper so you develop a continuous work action.

Fit a shaped nozzle onto the gun when stripping glazing bars to concentrate the jet of hot air and reduce the risk of cracking the glass.

Old primer can sometimes be difficult to remove with a hot air stripper. If you are repainting the timber this is no problem; just rub the surface down with abrasive paper. For a clear finish remove residues of paint from the grain with wads of wire wool dipped in chemical stripper (see left).

SEE ALSO

Details for:	▷
Preparing timber	27
Primers	21
Finishing wood	36–46

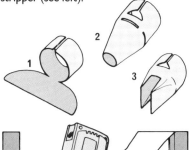

Nozzles for hot air guns
Hot air strippers come with a standard wide mouth for general usage but most offer optional extras, typically a push-on nozzle for stripping thin glazing bars (1) and a conical nozzle to concentrate the heat on a small area (2). Some offer nozzles for a wide spread of heat (3).

With a hot air gun there's less risk of scorching

METALWORK: IRON AND STEEL

Metal is a strong, hardwearing material that's used extensively throughout the home – for window frames, railings, gutters, pipework and radiators, to name but a few. Oddly, they're areas that are in close proximity to water, and consequently particularly prone to attack by metal's worst enemy: rust. Paint alone won't guard against this corrosive menace, so special treatments are necessary to ensure the long life of metal.

What is rust?

Rust is a form of corrosion that affects only the ferrous metals – notably iron and steel – due to the combination of water, oxygen and carbon dioxide. Although paint slows down the rate at which moisture penetrates, it doesn't stop it altogether; inhibitors and primers are needed to complete the protection, and the type you use depends on the condition of the metal and how you plan to decorate it. Prepare thoroughly or the job will be ruined.

Treating bare metal

Remove light deposits of rust by rubbing with wire wool or wet and dry abrasive paper dipped in white spirit. If the rust is heavy and the surface of the metal pitted, use a wire brush or, for extensive corrosion, a wire wheel or cup brush in a power drill. Wear goggles while wire brushing to protect your eyes from flying particles.

Paint a proprietary rust inhibitor onto the cleaned metal, following the manufacturer's instructions: some inhibitors remain on the surface to protect the metal, others must be washed off after a few minutes. Some car accessory shops carry a range of suitable inhibitors.

Wash off deposits of grease with white spirit and wire wool. As soon as the metal is clean and dry, apply a primer. For general inside use, choose a zinc phosphate or red oxide primer. For exterior paintwork, use calcium plumbate, red lead or zinc phosphate primers. Work the primer into crevices and fixings, and make sure sharp edges and corners where corrosion often begins are coated generously.

Cast iron railings deeply pitted with rust

Preparing previously painted metal

If the paint is perfectly sound, wash it with sugar soap or a detergent solution, rinse and dry. Key gloss paint with fine wet and dry abrasive.

If the paint film is blistered or flaking where water has penetrated and corrosion has set in, remove all loose paint and rust with a wire brush or rotary attachment to an electric drill. Apply rust inhibitor to bare patches, working it well into joints, bolt heads and other fixings. Prime bare metal immediately: rust can reform rapidly.

When you're preparing cast iron guttering, brush out dead leaves and other debris and wash it clean. Paint the inside with a bitumen paint. If you want to paint over old bitumen paint, use an aluminium primer first to prevent it bleeding to the surface.

Flaking casement window as a result of rust

Stripping painted metal

Delicately moulded sections – on fire surrounds, garden furniture and other cast or wrought ironwork – can't easily be rubbed down with a wire brush, and will often benefit from stripping off old paint and rust which is masking fine detail. A hot air stripper cannot be used here as the metal dissipates the heat before the paint softens. A gas blowtorch can be used to strip wrought ironwork, but cast iron might crack if it becomes distorted by localized heating.

Chemical stripping is the safest method but before you begin, check that what appears to be a metal fire surround is not in fact made from plaster mouldings on a wooden background: the stripping process can play havoc with soft plasterwork. Tap the surround to see if it is metallic, or scrape an inconspicuous section.

Apply a proprietary rust-killing jelly or liquid, chemicals which will remove and neutralize rust: usually based on phosphoric acid, they combine with the rust to leave it quite inert in the form of iron phosphate. Some rust killers will deal with minute particles invisible to the naked eye, and are self-priming, so no additional primer is required.

Alternatively, if the metalwork is portable, you can take it to a sandblaster or an industrial stripper (◁). None of the disadvantages of industrial stripping apply to metal.

Clean the stripped metal with a wire brush then wash with white spirit before finishing it.

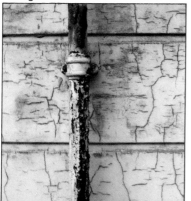

Severely corroded cast iron drainpipe

APPLYING FINISHES

A finish in decorating terms means a liquid or semi-liquid substance which sets, dries or cures to protect and sometimes colour materials such as wood or masonry. Apart from paint, other finishes for wood include stains, varnishes, oil, wax and French polish, all of which are used specifically where you want to display the grain of the timber for its natural beauty.

The make-up of paint

Paint is basically made from solid particles of pigment suspended in a liquid binder or medium. The pigment provides the colour and body of the paint, the medium allows the material to be brushed, rolled or sprayed and, once applied, forms a solid film binding the pigment together and adhering to the surface. Binder and pigment vary from paint to paint, but the commonest two families are solvent- (sometimes known as oil) and water-based.

SEE ALSO

Details for: ▷	
Choosing colours	6–7
Primers	21
Lead content	21
Preparing paint	32

Applying a paint system

No paint will provide protection for long if you apply one coat only. It is necessary to apply successive layers to build up a paint system.
● Paint for walls requires a simple system comprising two or three coats of the same paint.
● Paint intended for woodwork and metalwork needs a more complex system using paints with different qualities. A typical paint system for woodwork is illustrated below.

COMMON PAINT FINISHES AND ADDITIVES

The type of paint you choose depends on the finish you want and the material you're decorating. Various additives adapt the paint's qualities.

SOLVENT-BASED (OIL) PAINT

The medium for solvent-based paints (commonly called oil paints) is a mixture of oils and resin. A paint made from a natural resin is slow-drying, but modern paints contain synthetic resins such as alkyd, urea, epoxy, acrylic and vinyl, which all make for fast-drying paints. A white pigment, titanium dioxide, is added, plus other pigments to alter the colour.

WATER-BASED PAINT

Emulsion is the commonest water-based paint. It has a binder made from synthetic resins similar to those used for oil paints, but it is dispersed in a solution of water. Titanium is the white pigment used for good-quality paints. It is also used with additional pigments for a wide range of colours.

ADDITIVES IN PAINT

No paint is made from simply binder and pigment. Certain additives are included during manufacture to give the paint qualities such as faster drying, high gloss, easy flow, longer pot life, or to make the paint non-drip.
● **Thixotropic** paints are the typical non-drip types; they are thick, almost jelly-like in the can, enabling you to pick up a brush load without dripping.
● **Extenders** are added as fillers to strengthen the paint film. Cheap paint contains too much filler, reducing its covering power.

PAINT THINNERS

If a paint is too thick it cannot be applied properly and must be thinned before it is used. Some finishes require special thinners provided by the manufacturer, but most oil paints can be thinned with white spirit, and emulsions with water.
Turpentine will thin oil paint but has no advantages over white spirit for household paints and it is much more expensive.

GLOSS OR MATT FINISH?

The proportion of pigment to resin affects the way the paint sets. A gloss (shiny) paint contains approximately equal amounts of resin and pigment, whereas a higher proportion of pigment produces a matt (dull) paint. By adjusting the proportions, it is possible to make satin or eggshell paints. Matt paints tend to cover best due to their high pigment content, but the greater proportion of resin in gloss paints is responsible for their strength.

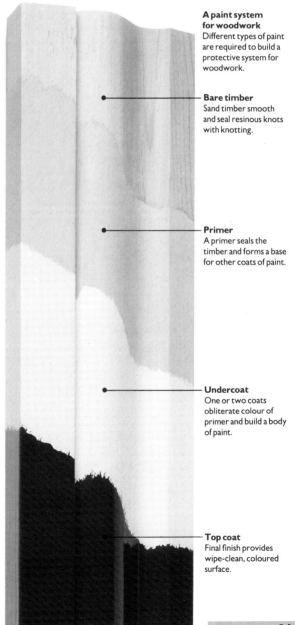

A paint system for woodwork
Different types of paint are required to build a protective system for woodwork.

Bare timber
Sand timber smooth and seal resinous knots with knotting.

Primer
A primer seals the timber and forms a base for other coats of paint.

Undercoat
One or two coats obliterate colour of primer and build a body of paint.

Top coat
Final finish provides wipe-clean, coloured surface.

SAFETY WHEN PAINTING

Decorating isn't dangerous so long as you take sensible precautions to protect your health.

- **Ensure good ventilation indoors while applying a finish and when it is drying. Wear a facemask if you have respiratory problems.**
- **Do not smoke while painting or in the vicinity of drying paint.**
- **Contain paint spillages outside with sand or earth and don't allow it to enter a drain.**
- **If you splash paint in your eyes, flush them with copious amounts of water with your lids held open; if symptoms persist, visit a doctor.**
- **Wear barrier cream or gloves on sensitive hands. Use a proprietary skin cleanser to remove paint from the skin or wash it off with warm soapy water. Do not use paint thinners to clean your skin.**
- **Keep any finish and thinners out of reach of children. If a child swallows a substance, do not attempt to make it vomit but seek medical treatment.**

SEE ALSO

◁ Details for:
Ladders and towers 18–20

PREPARING THE PAINT

Whether you're using newly purchased paint or leftovers from previous jobs, there are some basic rules to observe before you apply it.

- Wipe dust from the paint can, then prise off the lid with the side of a knife blade. Don't use a screwdriver: it only buckles the edge of the lid, preventing an airtight seal and making subsequent removal difficult.
- Gently stir liquid paints with a wooden stick to blend the pigment and medium. There's no need to stir thixotropic paints unless the medium has separated; if you have to stir it, leave it to gel again before using.
- If a skin has formed on paint, cut round the edge with a knife and lift out in one piece with a stick. It's a good idea to store the can on its lid, so that a skin cannot form on top of the paint.
- Whether the paint is old or new, transfer a small amount into a paint kettle or plastic bucket. Old paint should be filtered at the same time, tying a piece of muslin or old nylon tights across the rim of the kettle.

Strain old paint
If you're using leftover paint, filter it through a piece of muslin or old tights stretched over the rim of a container.

Resealing the lid
Wipe the rim of the can clean before you replace the lid, then tap it down all round with a hammer over a softwood block.

PAINTING EXTERIOR MASONRY

The outside walls of your house need painting for two major reasons: to give a clean, bright appearance and to protect the surface from the rigours of the climate. What you use as a finish and how you apply it depends on what the walls are made of, their condition and the degree of protection they need. Bricks are traditionally left bare, but may require a coat of paint if they're in bad condition or previous attempts to decorate have resulted in a poor finish. Rendered walls are normally painted to brighten the naturally dull grey colour of the cement; pebbledashed surfaces may need a colourful coat to disguise previous conspicuous patches. On the other hand, you may just want to change the present colour of your walls for a fresh appearance.

Working to a plan

Before you start painting the outside walls of your house, plan your time carefully. Depending on the preparation even a small house will take a few weeks to complete.

It's not necessary to tackle the whole job at once, although it is preferable – the weather may change to the detriment of your timetable. You can split the work into separate stages with days (even weeks) in between, so long as you divide the walls into manageable sections. Use window and door frames, bays, downpipes and corners of walls to form break lines that will disguise joins.

Start at the top of the house, working right to left if you are right-handed (vice versa if you are left-handed).

Black dot denotes compatibility. All surfaces must be clean, sound, dry and free from organic growth.

FINISHES FOR MASONRY	Cement paint	Exterior emulsion paint	Reinforced emulsion paint	Spirit-thinned masonry paint	Textured coating	Floor paint
SUITABLE TO COVER						
Brick	•	•	•	•	•	•
Stone	•	•	•	•	•	•
Concrete	•	•	•	•	•	•
Cement rendering	•	•	•	•	•	•
Pebbledash	•	•	•	•	•	•
Asbestos cement	•	•	•	•	•	•
Emulsion paint		•	•	•	•	
Oil-based paint		•	•	•	•	•
Cement paint	•	•	•	•	•	•
DRYING TIME: HOURS						
Touch dry	1-2	1-2	2-3	1-2	6	2-3
Re-coatable	24	4	24	24	24-48	12-24
THINNERS: SOLVENTS						
Water-thinned	•	•	•		•	
White spirit-thinned				•		•
NUMBER OF COATS						
Normal conditions	2	2	1-2	2	1	1-2
COVERAGE: DEPENDING ON WALL TEXTURE						
Sq.metres per litre		4-10	3-6.5	3-6		5-15
Sq.metres per kg	1.5-3.5				1-2	
METHOD OF APPLICATION						
Brush	•	•	•	•	•	•
Roller	•	•	•	•		•
Spray gun	•	•	•	•		•

Most interior walls and ceilings will be plastered and most probably papered or painted, unless the house has been recently built. Apart from their preparation, the methods for painting them are identical and they can be considered smooth surfaces in terms of paint coverage. Although a flat, matt finish is usually preferred indoors for walls and ceilings, there's no reason why you shouldn't use a gloss or even a textured paint in your scheme.

Finishes for bare masonry

Some interior walls are left unplastered – and some may even have been stripped on purpose – either for their decorative appearance or because it was considered unnecessary to clad the walls of certain rooms such as the basement, workshop or garage. A stripped brick or stone chimney breast makes an attractive focal point in a room, and an entire wall of bare masonry can create a dramatic effect or suggest a country cottage style.

If you want to finish brick, concrete or stone walls, follow the methods described for exterior walls. However, because they will not have to withstand weathering, you can use paint designed for interior use. Newly stripped masonry will require sealing to bind the surface (▷).

SEE ALSO

Details for:	▷
Primers and sealers	21
Stripping wallcoverings	24

SELECTING PAINTS FOR INTERIOR SURFACES

Although you really only have a choice of two finishes for interior walls and ceilings – emulsion or oil paint – there are various qualities which offer depth of sheen, texture, one-coat coverage and good obliteration.

EMULSION PAINT

The most popular and practical finish for walls and ceilings, emulsions are available in liquid or thixotropic consistencies with matt or satin (semi-gloss) finishes.

A satin finish emulsion is less likely to show fingerprints or scuffs. A non-drip, thixotropic paint has obvious advantages when painting ceilings, and covers in one coat. But apply a thinned coat on new, porous plaster, followed by a full-strength coat to achieve the required finish.

Emulsion is also available in a solid form, which comes in its own roller tray. It paints out well with minimal spatter and no drips.

REINFORCED EMULSION

Emulsion paints, reinforced with fine aggregate, are primarily for use on exterior walls but their fine textured finish is just as attractive inside and will cover minor imperfections, which would show through standard emulsions.

OIL PAINT

Oil paints dry to a hard, durable finish. Although these paints are mainly intended for woodwork, they can be used on walls that require an extra degree of protection: they were once popular in bathrooms and kitchens, where you might expect condensation, but this is unnecessary with the development of modern water-thinned emulsions, which resist moisture.

High-gloss paints accentuate uneven wall surfaces, so most people prefer a satin finish. Both types are available in liquid or thixotropic form. Most gloss paints should be preceded by one or two undercoats, but satin finishes, which have a very fine texture, form their own undercoats.

UNDERCOAT

Undercoat is a relatively cheap paint used to build up the full system of protective paintwork. It will obliterate underlying colours and fill minor irregularities. If speed is essential, choose a quick-drying primer/undercoat – a three-coat system of two undercoats and a top coat can be built up in one day.

CEMENT PAINT

Cement paint is an inexpensive exterior finish which is ideal for a utilitarian area indoors, such as a cellar, workshop or garage. Sold in dry powder form, it must be made up with water and dries to a matt finish.

Paints for walls and ceilings
Emulsion paint, in its many forms, is the most practical finish for interior walls and ceilings, but use oil paints on wall-fixed joinery like skirtings and picture rails. The example above illustrates the advantage of contrasting textures: matt emulsion for the cornice up to the ceiling; gloss oil paint for the picture rail; satin emulsion for the woodchip covered walls.

USING BRUSHES, PADS AND ROLLERS

Applying paint by brush

Choose a good-quality brush for painting walls and ceilings. Cheap brushes tend to shed bristles – infuriating and less economical in the long run. Buy a brush about 200mm (8in) wide for quickest coverage: if you're not used to handling a brush your wrist will soon tire and you may find a 150mm (6in) brush, plus a 50mm (2in) brush for the edges and corners, more comfortable to use, although take into account that the job will take longer.

Loading the brush

Don't overload a brush with paint; it leads to messy work and ruins the bristles if it is allowed to dry in the roots. Dip no more than the first third of the brush into the paint, wiping off excess on the side of the container to prevent drips (1). When using thixotropic paint, load the brush and apply paint without removing excess.

Using a brush

You can hold the brush whichever way feels comfortable to you, but the 'pen' grip is the most versatile, enabling your wrist to move the brush freely in any direction. Hold the brush handle between your thumb and forefinger, with your fingers on the ferrule (metal band) and your thumb supporting it from the other side (2).

Apply the paint in vertical strokes then spread it at right angles to even out the coverage. Emulsion paint will not show brush marks when it dries but finish oil paints with light upward vertical strokes for the best results.

1 Dip only the first third of bristles in paint

2 Place fingers on ferrule, thumb behind

Applying paint by roller

A paint roller with interchangeable sleeves is an excellent tool for applying paint to large areas. Choose a roller about 300mm (1ft) long for painting walls and ceilings.

There are a number of different sleeves to suit the type of paint and texture of the surface. Long-haired sheepskin and woven wool sleeves are excellent on texture surfaces, especially with emulsion paint. Choose a short-pile for smooth surfaces, and with oil paints.

Disposable plastic foam rollers can be used to apply any paint to a smooth surface but they soon lose their resilience and have a greater tendency to skid across the wall.

Special rollers

Rollers with long extension handles are designed for painting ceilings without having to erect a work platform (◁).

Some have a built-in paint reservoir for automatic reloading.

Narrow rollers are available for painting behind radiators, if you are unable to remove them (◁).

Loading a roller

You will need a special paint tray to load a standard roller. Having dipped the sleeve lightly into the paint reservoir, roll it gently onto the ribbed part of the tray to coat the roller evenly (1).

Using a roller

Use zig-zag strokes with a roller (2), covering the surface in all directions. Keep it on the surface at all times. If you let it spin at the end of a stroke it will spray paint onto the floor or adjacent surface. When applying oil paint, finish in one direction, preferably towards prevailing light.

● **Spraying**
It is possible to spray paint onto interior walls and ceilings, but it is only practical for large rooms: you'll have to mask everything you don't want to paint; and the sprayed paint would be forced through even the narrowest gaps between doors and frames. Adequate ventilation is vital when spraying indoors.

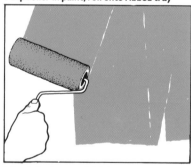

1 Dip roller in paint, roll onto ribbed tray

2 Apply in zig-zags, finish in one direction

Applying paint by pad

Paint pads for large surfaces have flat rectangular faces covered with a short mohair pile. A plastic foam backing gives the pad flexibility so that the pile will always be in contact with the wall, even on a rough surface.

The exact size of the pad will be determined by the brand you choose but one about 200mm (8in) long is best for applying paint evenly and smoothly to walls and ceilings. You will also need a small pad or paintbrush for cutting in at corners and ceilings.

Loading a pad

Load a pad from its own special tray, drawing the pad across the captive roller so that you pick up an even amount of paint (1).

Using a pad

To apply the paint consistently, keep the pad flat on the wall and sweep it gently and evenly in any direction (2). Use criss-cross strokes for emulsion, but finish with vertical strokes with oil paints to prevent streaking.

1 Loading a paint pad
Load the pad evenly by drawing it across the integral roller on the tray without squeezing.

2 Sweep pad gently in any direction

Even the most experienced painter can't help dripping a little paint, so always paint a ceiling before the wall, especially if they are to be different colours. Erect a work platform so that you can cover as much of the surface as possible without having to change position: you will achieve a better finish and will be able to work in safety. When you start to paint, follow a strict working routine to ensure a faultless finish. Choose your tools wisely so you can work efficiently. Refer to the chart below for professional results.

Painting the ceiling

Start in a corner near the window and carefully paint along the edges with a small paintbrush.

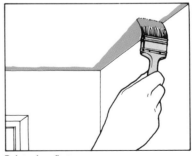

Paint edges first

Working from the wet edges, paint in 600mm (2ft) wide bands, working away from the light. Whether you use a brush, a pad or a roller, apply each fresh load of paint just clear of the previous application, blending in the junctions for even coverage.

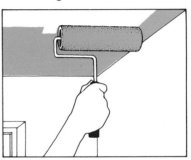

Work from wet edges

● Black dot denotes compatibility. All surfaces must be clean, sound, dry and free from organic growth.

FINISHES FOR INTERIOR WALLS & CEILINGS

	Emulsion paint	Reinforced emulsion paint	Oil-based paints	Undercoat	Primer/ undercoat	Cement paint	Textured coating
SUITABLE TO COVER							
Plaster	●	●	●	●	●	●	●
Wallpaper	●		●	●	●		
Brick	●	●	●		●	●	●
Stone	●	●	●		●	●	●
Concrete	●	●	●		●	●	●
Previously painted surface	●	●		●	●		●
DRYING TIME: HOURS							
Touch dry	1-2	2-3	4	4	½	1-2	6
Re-coatable	4	24	16	16	2	24	24-48
THINNERS: SOLVENTS							
Water	●	●				●	●
White spirit			●	●	●		
NUMBER OF COATS							
Normal conditions	2	1-2	1-2	1-2	1-2	2	1
COVERAGE: APPROXIMATE							
Sq. metres per litre	9-15	3-6.5	12-17	15-18	15		
Sq. metres per kg						1.5-3.5	1-2
METHOD OF APPLICATION							
Brush	●	●	●	●	●	●	●
Roller	●	●	●	●	●	●	●
Paint pad	●		●	●	●	●	
Spray	●	●	●	●	●	●	

Electrical fittings

Unscrew a ceiling rose cover so that you can paint right up to the backplate with a small brush. Loosen the faceplate or mounting box of sockets and switches to paint behind them.

Remember: switch off at the mains before exposing electrical connections (▷).

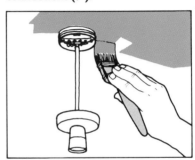

Unscrew rose cover to keep it clean

Paint reservoir
Use a special roller with a pressurized paint reservoir to avoid having to constantly reload a roller; it's an excellent boon for painting ceilings and high walls, when frequent returns to the tray would be tiresome.

Painting the walls

Use a small brush to paint the edges starting at a top corner of the room. If you are right-handed, work right to left. Paint an area of about 600mm (2ft) square at a time. If you are left-handed, paint the wall in the opposite direction. When using emulsion, paint in horizontal bands **(1)**, but, with oil paints, use vertical strips **(2)** as the junctions are more likely to show unless you blend in the wet edges quickly. Always finish a complete wall before you take a break or a change of tone will show between separate painted sections.

1 Paint emulsion in horizontal bands

2 Apply oil paints in vertical strips

FINISHING WOODWORK

Paint is the usual finish for woodwork in and around the house – it gives a protective, decorative coating and there's a vast choice of colours and surface finishes. But stains, varnishes or polishes can also be used not just for furniture but as an attractive, durable finish for joinery. They enable you to add colour to woodwork without obliterating the natural beauty of its grain; transparent finishes are also a good alternative where you don't want to alter the natural wood colour. Bear in mind the location of the woodwork and the amount of wear it is likely to get when choosing a finish.

Left to right
1 Wax polish
2 Coloured preserver
3 Satin oil paint
4 Cold cure lacquer
5 Gloss oil paint
6 Oil finish
7 Unsealed wood stain
8 Opaque microporous wood stain
9 Clear microporous wood stain
10 Polyurethane varnish

The list below comprises a comprehensive range of finishes available for decorating and protecting woodwork in and around the house. Each finish has qualities particular to its intended usage, although many can be used simply for their attractive appearance rather than for any practical considerations – this, however, depends on the location of timberwork, as some finishes are much more durable than others.

OIL PAINT

Oil (solvent-based) paints are still the most popular finish, primarily for the range of colours offered by all paint manufacturers, secondarily because they last for many years with only the occasional wash down to remove finger marks. Outside, their durability is reduced considerably due to the combined action of sun and rain: consider redecoration every two or three years. They are available as a gloss or satin finish with both liquid and thixotropic consistencies.

One or two undercoats are essential, especially for outside.

GLOSS EMULSION PAINT

Emulsion-based gloss paint was introduced by several manufacturers but is still quite rare. Beneficially, it dries much faster than oil paint and without the strong smell associated with such paint. It is suitable for both interior and exterior use. It allows moisture to escape from the wood while protecting it from rainwater – which oil paint does not – so reduces the risk of flaking and blistering. Gloss emulsion requires its own compatible primer/undercoat. The usual system of two undercoats and one top coat can be applied in one day.

WOOD STAIN

Unlike paint, which after the initial priming coat rests on the surface of timber, stain penetrates the wood. Its main advantage is to enhance the natural colour of the woodwork or to unify the slight variation in colour found in even the same species.

Water- or oil-based stains are available ready for use but powdered pigments are available for mixing with methylated spirit. None of these stains will actually protect the timber and you will have to seal them with a clear varnish or polish.

There are protective wood stains (often sold as *microporous paints* or *breathing paints*) specially made for use on exterior joinery. The microporous nature of the coating allows water to escape from the wood, yet provides a weather-resistant satin finish. Being a stain, it does not crack, peel or flake. Choose a semi-transparent stain when you want the grain to show, or an opaque one for less attractive timbers.

COLOURED PRESERVERS

Sawn timber fencing, wall cladding and outbuildings look particularly unattractive when painted, yet they need protection. Use a wood preserver, which penetrates deeply into the timber to prevent rot and insect attack ($\triangleright$). There are clear preservers, plus a range of browns and greens, and usually one for red cedar.

Traditional preservers such as creosote have a strong, unpleasant smell and are harmful to plants, but there are several organic solvent preservers, which are perfectly safe – even for greenhouses and propagators.

VARNISH

Varnish is a clear protective coating for timber. Most modern varnishes are made with polyurethane resins to provide a waterproof scratch- and heat-resistant finish. The majority are ready to apply, although some are supplied with a catalyst, which must be added before the varnish is used. These two-component varnishes are even tougher than standard polyurethanes and are especially suitable for treating wooden floors: you can choose from high gloss, satin or matt.

An exterior grade of varnish is more weather-resistant. Yacht varnish, which is formulated to withstand even salt water, would be an ideal finish for exterior woodwork in a coastal climate.

Coloured varnishes are designed to provide a stain and clear finish at the same time. They are available in the normal wood shades and some strong primary colours. Unlike a true stain, a coloured varnish does not sink into the timber, so there is a possibility of a local loss of colour in areas of heavy wear or abrasion unless you apply additional coats of clear varnish.

COLD CURE LACQUER

Cold cure lacquer is a plastic coating, which is mixed with a hardener just before it is used. It is extremely durable, even on floors, and is heat- and alcohol-resistant. The standard type dries to a high gloss, which can be burnished to a lacquer-like finish if required. There is also a matt finish grade but a smoother matt surface can be obtained by rubbing down the gloss coating with fine steel wool and wax. It is available in clear, black or white.

OIL

Oil is a subtle finish which soaks into the wood, leaving a mellow sheen on the surface. Traditional linseed oils remain sticky for hours but a modern oil will dry in about one hour and provides a tougher, more durable finish. Oil can be used on softwood as well as open-grained oily hardwoods, such as teak or afrormosia. It is suitable for interior and exterior woodwork.

WAX POLISH

Wax can be used as a dressing to preserve and maintain another finish, or it can be used as a finish itself. A good wax should be a blend of beeswax and a hard polishing wax such as carnauba. Some contain silicones to make it easier to achieve a high gloss.

Polishes are white or tinted to various shades of brown to darken the wood. Although it is attractive, wax polish is not a durable finish and should be used indoors only.

FRENCH POLISH

French polish is made by dissolving shellac in alcohol and if properly applied, can be burnished to a mirror-like finish. It is easily scratched and alcohol, or even water, will etch the surface, leaving white stains. Consequently, it can be used only on furniture unlikely to receive normal wear and tear.

There are several varieties of shellac polish. Button polish is the best quality standard polish and is reddish brown in colour. It is bleached to make white polish for light coloured woods and if the natural wax is removed from the shellac, a clear, transparent polish is produced. For mahogany, choose a darker red garnet polish.

SEE ALSO

Details for:	$\triangleright$
Wood-boring insects	78
Primers	21

PAINTING WOODWORK

When you're painting wood, take into account that it's a fibrous material, which has a definite grain pattern, different rates of absorbency, knots that may ooze resin – all qualities that influence the type of paint you use and the techniques and tools you'll need to apply it.

Basic application

Prepare and prime all new woodwork thoroughly (◁) before applying the final finish. If you are using gloss paint, apply one or two undercoats, depending on the covering power of the paint. As each coat hardens, rub down with fine wet and dry paper to remove blemishes and wipe the surface with a cloth dampened with white spirit.

Best quality paintbrushes are the most efficient tools for painting woodwork. You will need 25mm (1in) and 50mm (2in) brushes for general work and a 12mm (½in) paintbrush for painting narrow glazing bars. Apply the paint with vertical strokes then spread sideways to even out the coverage. Finish with light strokes – called laying off – in the direction of the grain. Blend the edges of the next application while the paint is still wet, or a hard edge will show. Don't go back over a painted surface that has started to dry, or it will leave a blemish in the surface.

It is not necessary to spread thixotropic paint in the same way. Simply lay on the paint in almost parallel strokes leaving the brush strokes to settle out naturally.

● **Removing a blemish**
If you find specks of fluff or a brush bristle embedded in fresh paintwork, don't attempt to remove them once a skin has begun to form on the paint. Let it harden then rub down with wet and dry paper. The same applies if you discover runs.

Painting a panel
When painting up to the edge of a panel, brush from the centre out: if you flex the bristles against the edge, the paint will run.

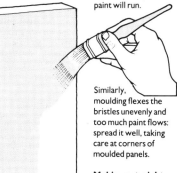

Similarly, moulding flexes the bristles unevenly and too much paint flows: spread it well, taking care at corners of moulded panels.

Making a straight edge
To finish an area with a straight edge, use one of the smaller brushes and place it a few millimetres from the edge. As you flex the bristles, they'll spread to the required width, laying on an even coat of paint.

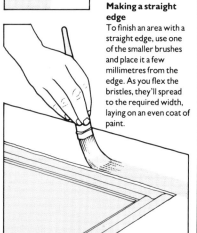

THE ORDER OF WORK

Follow the sequences recommended below for painting interior and exterior woodwork successfully:

INSIDE

Start painting windows early in the day, so you can close them at night without the new film sticking. Paint doors, then picture rails; finish with skirting boards so that any specks of dust picked up on the brush won't be transferred to other areas.

OUTSIDE

Choose the order of painting according to the position of the sun. Avoid painting in direct sunlight as this will cause glare with light colours and results in runs or blistering. Never paint on wet or windy days: rain specks will pit the finish and airborne dust will ruin the surface. Paint windows and exterior doors early, so that they are touch-dry by the evening.

FINISHES FOR WOODWORK

● Black dot denotes compatibility. All surfaces must be clean, sound, dry and free from organic growth.

	Oil paint	Gloss emulsion	Wood stain	Protective wood stain	Coloured preserver	Varnish	Coloured varnish	Cold cure lacquer	Oil	Wax polish	French polish
SUITABLE FOR											
Softwoods	●	●	●	●	●	●	●	●	●	●	
Hardwoods	●	●	●	●	●	●	●	●	●	●	●
Oily hardwoods	●	●	●	●	●	●	●	●	●	●	●
Planed wood	●	●	●	●	●	●	●	●	●	●	
Sawn wood				●	●						
Interior use	●	●	●	●		●	●	●	●	●	●
Exterior use	●	●		●	●	●			●		
DRYING TIME: HOURS											
Touch-dry	4	1	½	4	1-2	4	4	1	1		½
Re-coatable	14	3	6	6-8	2-4	14	14	2	6	1	24
THINNERS: SOLVENTS											
Water		●			●						
White spirit	●		●	●	●	●	●		●	●	
Methylated spirit											●
Special thinner								●			
NUMBER OF COATS											
Interior use	1-2	1-2	2-3	2		2-3	2-3	2-3	3	2	10-15
Exterior use	2-3	1-2		2	2	3-4	3-4		3		
COVERAGE											
Sq metres per litre	12-16	10-15	16-30	10-25	4-12	15-16	15-16	16-17	10-15	VARIABLE	VARIABLE
METHOD OF APPLICATION											
Brush	●	●	●	●	●	●	●	●	●	●	●
Paint pad	●	●	●	●	●	●	●		●		
Cloth pad (rubber)			●			●	●		●		●
Spray gun	●	●		●	●	●	●	●			

PAINTING DOORS

Doors have a variety of faces and conflicting grain patterns that need to be painted separately – yet the end result must look even in colour without ugly brush marks or heavily painted edges. There's a strict system for painting panel, flush or glazed doors.

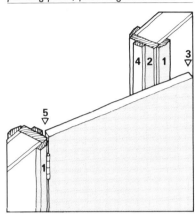

Painting each side a different colour
Make sure all the surfaces that face you when the door is open are painted the same colour.

Opening side: paint the architrave (**1**) and door frame up to and including the edge of the door stop (**2**) one colour. Paint the face of the door and its opening edge (**3**) the same colour.

Opposite side: paint the architrave and frame up to and over the door stop (**4**) the second colour. Paint the opposite face of the door and its hinged edge (**5**) with the second colour.

Preparation and technique

Remove the door handles and wedge the door open so that it cannot be closed accidentally, locking you in the room. Keep the handle in the room with you, just in case.

Aim to paint the door and its frame separately so that there is less chance of touching wet paintwork when passing through a freshly painted doorway. Paint the door first and when it is dry finish the framework.

If you want to use a different colour for each side of the door, paint the hinged edge the colour of the closing face (the one that comes to rest against the frame). Paint the outer edge of the door the same colour as the opening face. This means that there won't be any difference in colour when viewed from either side.

Each side of the frame should match the corresponding face of the door. When painting in the room into which the door swings, paint that side of the frame, including the edge of the stop bead against which the door closes, to match the opening face. Paint the rest of the frame the colour of the closing face.

System for a flush door

To paint a flush door, start at the top and work down in sections, blending each one into the other. Lay on the paint, then finish each section with light vertical brush strokes. Finally, paint the edges. Brush from edges, never onto them, or the paint will build up, run and a ridge will form.

System for a panel door

The different parts of a panelled door must be painted in logical order. Finish each part with parallel strokes in the direction of the grain.

Whatever the style of panelled door you are painting, start with the mouldings (**1**) followed by the panels (**2**). Paint the centre verticals – muntins (**3**) next, then the cross rails (**4**).

Finish the face by painting the outer verticals – stiles (**5**). Paint the edge of the door (**6**).

To achieve a superior finish, paint the muntins, rails and stiles together, picking up the wet edges of paint before they begin to dry, show brush strokes and pull out bristles. To get the best results you must work quickly.

SEE ALSO

Details for: ▷	
Glazing bars	40
Primers	21
Preparing wood	27
Preparing paintwork	28
Staining a door	43

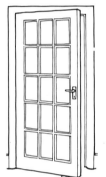

Glazed doors
To paint a glazed door, begin with the glazing bars (▷) then follow the sequence as described for panel doors.

Flush door
Apply square sections of paint, working down from the top, and pick up the wet edges for a good blend. Lay off with light vertical brush strokes.

Panel door: basic painting method
Follow the numbered sequence for painting the various parts of the door, each finished with strokes along the grain to prevent streaking.

Panel door: advanced painting method
Working rapidly, follow the alternative sequence to produce a finish free from joins between sections.

Flush door

Panel door – basic method

Panel door – advanced method

● **Clean windows first**
Clean the glass in your windows before decorating to avoid picking up particles of dust in the paint.

Cutting-in brush
Paint glazing bars with a cutting-in brush, which has its bristles cut at an angle to enable you to work right up to the glass with a thin line of paint.

● **Painting French windows**
Although French windows are really glazed doors, treat them like large casement windows.

PROTECTING THE GLASS

When painting the edge of glazing bars, overlap the glass by about 2mm (1/16in) to prevent rain or condensation seeping between the glass and woodwork.

If you find it difficult to achieve a satisfactory straight edge, use a proprietary plastic or metal paint shield held against the edge of the frame to protect the glass.

Alternatively, run masking tape around the edges of the window pane, leaving a slight gap so that the paint will seal the join between glass and frame. When the paint is touch-dry, carefully peel off the tape. Don't wait until the paint is completely dry or the film may peel off with the tape.

Scrape off any paint accidentally dripped onto the glass using a razor blade, once it has set. Plastic handles to hold blades are sold by many DIY stores for this purpose.

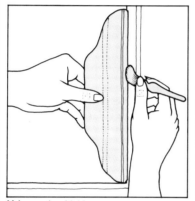

Using a paint shield
A plastic or metal paint shield enables you to paint a straight edge up to glass.

KEEPING THE WINDOW OPEN

With the catch and stay removed there's nothing to stop the frame closing. Make a stay with a length of stiff wire, hook the other end and slot it into one of the screw holes in the frame.

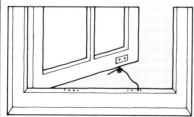

Temporary stay
Wind wire around a nail driven in the underside of the frame and use as a stay.

PAINTING WINDOW FRAMES

Window frames need to be painted in strict order, like doors, so that the various components will be evenly treated and so that you can close them at night. You *also need to take care not to splash panes with paint or apply a crooked line around the glazing bars – the mark of poor workmanship.*

Painting a casement window

A casement window hinges like a door, so if you plan to paint each side a different colour, follow a similar procedure to that described for painting doors and frames.

Remove the stay and catch before you paint the window. So that you can still operate the window during decorating without touching wet paint, drive a nail into the underside of the bottom rail as a makeshift handle.

Painting sequence
First paint the glazing bars (1), cutting into the glass on both sides. Carry on with the top and bottom horizontal rails (2) followed by the vertical stiles (3). Finish the casement by painting the edges (4) then paint the frame (5).

Painting sequence for casement window ▷

Painting a sash window

Sash windows are the most difficult type to paint, as the two panes slide vertically, overlapping each other.

The following sequence describes the painting of a sash window from the inside. To paint the outside face, use a similar procedure but start with the lower sash. When using different colours for each side, the demarcation lines are fairly obvious. When the window is closed, all the visible surfaces from one side should be the same.

Painting sequence
Raise the bottom sash and pull down the top one. Paint the bottom meeting rail of the top sash (1) and the accessible parts of the vertical members (2). Reverse the position of the sashes, leaving a gap top and bottom and complete the painting of the top sash (3). Paint the bottom sash (4) then the frame (5) except for the runners in which the sashes slide.

Leave the paint to dry then paint the inner runners (6) plus a short section of the outer runners (7). When painting the runners, pull the cords aside to avoid splashing paint on them, as this will make them brittle, shortening their working life. Make sure the window slides before the paint dries.

Raise bottom sash and pull down top

Reverse the position of the sashes

Lower both sashes for access to runners

PAINTING FIXED JOINERY

Staircase
Paint banisters first, making sure that you do not precipitate runs by stroking the brush against the edges or mouldings. Start at the top of the stairs, painting the treads, risers and strings (▷) together to keep the edges of the paintwork fresh.

If there is any chance that the paint will not dry before the staircase is used again, paint all risers but alternate treads only. The next day, paint the remainder.

Skirting boards
The only problem with painting a skirting board is to protect the floor from paint and at the same time avoid picking up dust on the wet paintbrush.

Slide strips of thin card under the skirting as a paint shield (don't use newspaper; it will tear and remain stuck to the skirting).

PAINTING EXTERIOR WEATHERBOARDING

Start at the top of the wall and apply paint to one or two boards at a time. Paint the under-edge first, then the face of the boards; finish parallel with the edge. Make sure you coat exposed end grain well, as it is more absorbent and requires extra protection.

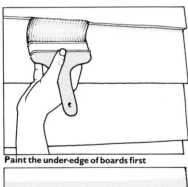
Paint the under-edge of boards first

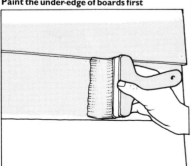
Paint the face of boards next

GRAINING TIMBER

Graining is a technique for simulating natural wood with paint. It was used extensively on cheap softwood joinery to imitate expensive hardwoods. Doors and panels can look attractive treated in this way. The basic method is simple to describe but practice on a flat board is essential before you can achieve convincing results. A skilled grainer can simulate actual species of timber, but just try to suggest ordinary wood grain rather than attempt to produce a perfect copy.

Equipment and preparation for graining

The simplest graining effects can be achieved by removing dark paint to reveal a paler basecoat below. The traditional way to carry out this effect is to use a special hog's- or squirrel's-hair brush called a mottler or grainer. To compromise, try any soft-bristled paintbrush or even a dusting brush. You can also buy steel, rubber or leather combs from decorator's suppliers to achieve similar effects.

Applying a basecoat (ground)
Prepare the basecoat as normal paintwork, finishing with a satin oil paint. It should represent the lightest colour of the timber you want to reproduce and is normally beige or olive green. The basecoat will look more convincing if it is slightly dull rather than being too bright.

Choosing the graining colour
Translucent, flat-drying paints are produced especially for graining in a range of appropriate colours. These paints must be thinned with a mixture comprising 2 parts white spirit: 1 part raw linseed oil to make a graining glaze. The quantity of thinners controls the colour of the graining, so add it to the paint sparingly until you achieve the required result. Try the method on a practice panel first.

Producing the effect

Paint an even coat of glaze onto the ground with a 50mm (2in) paintbrush. After only two or three minutes, lightly drag the tip of the mottler or comb along the line of the rail or panel, leaving faint streaks in the glaze.

When two rails meet at right-angles, mask the joint with a piece of card to prevent the simulated grain being disturbed on one rail while you paint a rail next to it.

The grain does not have to be exactly parallel with the rail. You can vary the pattern by allowing the comb or mottler to streak out the glaze at a slight angle and over the edge of some of the rails.

Leave the graining to dry overnight then apply one or two coats of clear varnish to protect and seal the effects.

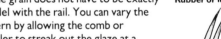

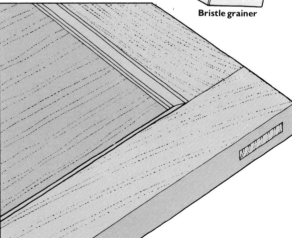
Masking meeting rails
Hold a piece of card over the joint between two meeting rails – on a panel door, for instance, where muntins meet cross rails – to prevent spoiling the graining effect on one while you treat the other.

Applying graining patterns
Produce graining patterns that are as authentic as possible. Don't just run the streaks in one direction, or parallel to the timber: simulate actual wood grain by running the pattern at an angle.

Steel graining comb

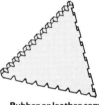
Rubber or leather comb

Bristle grainer

41

STAINING WOODWORK

Unless the wood is perfectly clean and free from grease, the stain will be rejected, producing an uneven, patchy appearance. Strip any previous finish and sand the wood with progressively finer abrasive papers, always in the direction of the grain. Scratches made across the grain will tend to be emphasized by the stain.

Testing the stain
Make a test strip (far right) to assess the depth of colour of various stains before embarking on the final job. Apply a band of varnish along the bottom half of the strip to see how the colours are affected.

Paint pad

Paintbrush

Rubber

Making a test strip

The final colour is affected by the nature of the timber, the number of coats and the overlying clear finish. You can also mix compatible stains to alter the colour or dilute them with the appropriate thinner.

Make a test strip so that you will have an accurate guide from which you can choose the depth of stain to suit your purpose. Use a piece of timber from the same batch you are staining, or one that resembles it closely.

Paint the whole strip with one coat of stain. Allow the stain to be absorbed then apply a second coat, leaving a strip of the first application showing. It is rarely necessary to apply more than two coats of stain, but for the experiment add a third and even a fourth coat, always leaving a strip of the previous application for comparison.

When the stain has dried completely, paint a band of clear varnish along the strip: some polyurethane varnishes react unfavourably with oil-based stains, so it is advisable to use products made by the same manufacturer.

USING A RUBBER

Wear gloves to protect your skin and pour some stain into a shallow dish. Saturate the rubber with stain then squeeze some out so that it is not dripping but still wet enough to apply a liberal coat of stain to the surface.

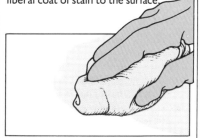

Apply stain by rubber

If you wet a piece of timber, water is absorbed by the wood, raising a mass of tiny fibres across the surface. A water-based stain will produce the same result and the final finish will be ruined. Solve the problem by sanding the wood until it is perfectly smooth, then dampen the whole surface with a wet rag. Leave it to dry out then sand the raised grain with very fine abrasive paper before you apply the stain. If you are using an oil-based stain, this preliminary process is unnecessary.

If you want to fill the grain, first apply a seal coat of clear finish over the stain. Choose a grain filler that matches the stain closely, adjusting the colour by adding a little stain to it, but make sure that the stain and filler are compatible. An oil-based stain will not mix with a water-based filler and vice versa, so check before you buy either.

How to apply wood stain

Use a 100mm (4in) paintbrush to apply stains over a wide, flat surface. Do not brush out a stain like paint, but apply it liberally and evenly, always in the direction of the grain.

It is essential to blend wet edges of stain, so work fairly quickly and don't take a break until you have completed the job. If you have brushed a water-based stain onto the wood it is sometimes advantageous to wipe over the wet surface with a soft cloth and remove excess stain.

A paint pad is one of the best applicators for achieving an even coverage of wood stain over a flat surface. However, you may find that you will still need a paintbrush to get the stain into awkward corners and for tackling mouldings.

Because stains are so fluid, it's often easier to apply them with a wad of soft, lint-free rag called a rubber (◁). You'll be able to control runs on a vertical panel and it's the best way to stain turned wood and rails.

STAINING PANELS, FLOORS AND DOORS

Staining a flat panel

Whenever possible, set up a panel horizontally for staining, either on trestles or raised on softwood blocks. Shake the container before use and pour the stain into a flat dish so that you can load your applicator properly.

Apply the stain, working swiftly and evenly along the grain. Stain the edges at the same time as the top surface. The first application may have a slightly patchy appearance as it dries because some parts of the wood will absorb more stain than others. The second coat normally evens out the colour without difficulty. If powdery deposits are left on the surface of the dry stain, wipe them off with a coarse, dry cloth, before applying the second coat in the same way as the first.

Leave the stain to dry overnight then proceed with the clear finish of your choice to seal the colourant.

Staining floors

Because a wooden floor is such a large area it is more difficult to blend the wet edges of the stain. Work along two or three boards at a time, using a paintbrush, so that you can finish at the edge of a board each time.

Wood block floors are even trickier, so try to complete one panel at a time, and use a soft cloth to blend in any overlapping areas.

Staining a door

Stain a new or stripped door before it is hung so that it can be layed horizontally. A flush door is stained just like any other panel but use a rubber to carefully colour the edges so that stain does not run under to spoil the other side.

When staining a panelled door, it is essential to follow a sequence which will allow you to pick up the edges of stain before they dry. Use a combination of brush and rubber to apply the stain.

Follow the numbered sequence below and note that, unlike painting a panel door, the mouldings are stained last – this is to prevent any overlapping showing on the finished door. Stain the mouldings carefully with a narrow brush and blend in the colour with a rubber.

Method for staining a panel door
Follow this practical sequence, using a combination of paintbrush or paint pad and rubber to apply the stain evenly to the various sections. Start with the inset panels first (1), then continue with half of the centre vertical rail (2), the bottom cross rail (3) and half the stiles (4). Pick up the wet edges with the other half of the centre vertical (5) and the stiles (6). Stain the centre cross rail (7), then repeat the procedure for the second half of the door (8-12), finishing with the mouldings (13) using a narrow brush and rubber.

● **Pads for mouldings**
Although paint pads are excellent for laying on flat areas of stain, they can be awkward to use on moulded woodwork, particularly when staining glazed bars. However, small pads are made specifically for this purpose.

USING WOOD STAINS OUTSIDE

Standard wood stains are not suitable for exterior use. They have no protective properties of their own and they have a tendency to fade in direct sunlight. For planed joinery and weatherboarding, use a microporous protective wood stain (▷). For sawn timber use a coloured wood preserver. Both materials are much thinner than paint, so take care to avoid splashing.

Protective wood stain
Make sure the surface is clean, dry and sanded. All previous paint or varnish must be stripped. For blemished timber, use an opaque wood stain so that you can fill cracks and holes. For extra protection treat the timber with a clear wood preserver before staining.

Apply two coats with a paintbrush, making sure that the coating is even, and avoid any overlaps.

Stain wall cladding one board at a time (treating the under-edge first).

Wood preserver
Before you apply wood preserver, remove surface dirt with a stiff-bristled brush. Paint or varnish must be stripped completely, but previously preserved or creosoted timber can be treated, so long as it has weathered.

For additional protection against insect and fungal attack, treat the timber first with a clear wood preserver, either by immersion or by full brush coats (▷).

Paint a full coat of coloured preserver onto the wood followed by a second coat as soon as the first has soaked in. Brush out sufficiently to achieve an even colour and avoid overlaps by following immediately with the edges of boards, rails and posts.

Replacing putty
Stain will not colour putty. In any case, microporous stains allow the wood to breathe, so there's likely to be some movement, which puts greater strain on the glass. For both reasons, remove the old putty and stain the frame. Seal the rebate with mastic (1).

Set lengths of stained wooden beading into the mastic and secure them with panel pins (2). You'll find it easiest to fix the beading if you tap in the pins beforehand, so they just protrude through the other side. Remove excess mastic squeezed from beneath the beading with a putty knife (3).

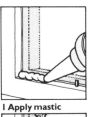

I **Apply mastic**

2 **Fix beading**

3 **Trim mastic**

VARNISHING WOODWORK

Varnish serves two main purposes: to protect the wood from knocks, stains and other marks, and to give it a sheen that accentuates the beautiful grain pattern. In some cases, it can even be used to change the colour of the wood to that of another species – or to give it a fresh, new look with a choice of bright primary colours.

The effect of varnish
The example below demonstrates how different varnishes affect the same species of wood. From top to bottom: untreated birch plywood; matt clear varnish; gloss clear varnish; wood shade coloured varnish; pure coloured varnish.

How to apply varnish

Use paintbrushes to apply varnish in the same way as paint. You will need a range of sizes for general work: 12mm (½in), 25mm (1in) and 50mm (2in) are useful widths. For varnishing floors use a 100mm (4in) brush for quick coverage. With any brush, make sure it's spotlessly clean; any previous traces of paint may mar the finish.

Load a brush with varnish by dipping the first third of the bristles into the liquid, then touch off the excess on the side of the container. Don't scrape the brush across the rim of the container as it causes bubbles in the varnish, which can spoil the finish if transferred to the woodwork.

A soft cloth pad, or rubber (◁) can be used to apply the first coat of varnish into the grain. It is not essential to use a rubber – even for the sealing coat – but it is a convenient method, especially for coating shaped or turned pieces of wood.

Applying the varnish

Thin the first coat of varnish with 10 per cent white spirit and rub it well into the wood with a cloth pad in the direction of the grain. Brush on the sealer coat where the rubber is difficult to use.

Apply the second coat of varnish not less than six hours later. If more than 24 hours have elapsed, key the surface of gloss varnish lightly with fine abrasive paper. Wipe it over with a cloth dampened with white spirit to remove dust and grease, then brush on a full coat of varnish as for paint.

Apply a third coat if the surface is likely to take hard wear.

Using coloured varnish

A wood stain can only be used on bare timber, but you can use a coloured varnish to darken or alter the colour of woodwork that has been varnished previously without having to strip the finish. Clean the surface with wire wool and white spirit mixed with a little linseed oil (◁). Dry the surface with a clean cloth then apply the varnish.

Apply tinted varnish in the same way as the clear type. It might be worth making a test strip to see how many coats you will need to achieve the depth of colour you want (◁).

Varnishing floors

Varnishing a floor is no different to finishing any other woodwork but the greater area can produce an unpleasant concentration of fumes in a confined space. Open all windows for ventilation and wear a gauze facemask.

Start in the corner furthest from the door and work back towards it. Brush the varnish out well to make sure it does not collect in pools.

DEALING WITH DUST PARTICLES

Minor imperfections and particles of dust stuck to the varnished surface can be rubbed down with fine abrasive paper between coats. If your top coat is to be a high-gloss finish, take even more care to ensure that your brush is perfectly clean.

If you are not satisfied with your final finish, dip very fine wire wool in wax polish and rub the varnish with parallel strokes in the direction of the grain. Buff the surface with a soft duster. This will remove the high gloss but it leaves a pleasant sheen on the surface with no obvious imperfections.

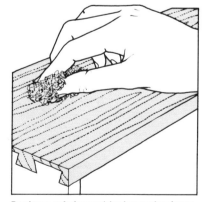

Produce a soft sheen with wire wool and wax

FRENCH POLISHING

The art of French polishing has always been considered the province of the expert, which a wise amateur would leave well alone. It is true that an expert will make a better job of the polishing and can work much faster than an amateur, but there's no reason why anyone cannot produce a satisfactory finish with a little practice.

Basic French polishing

Try out French polishing using one of the prepared proprietary kits available from DIY stores. A kit typically contains a bottle of thin shellac for building up the body of polish and a separate clear burnishing liquid.

Brush coating

Pour some shellac into a shallow dish so that you can use a brush to paint the polish onto the wood. Keep the coating even and work quickly to pick up the moist edges. Don't go over an area more than once.

Half an hour later, brush coat the work again then leave it for another hour. Next, lightly sand the polish with a silicon carbide paper (grey with a dry lubricant embedded in its surface) to remove any blemishes.

Building up the polish

With the workpiece set up at a comfortable working height and in good light, distribute the polish along the surface of the wood with continuous, circular strokes of the rubber.

There's no need to press too hard at first as a fully charged rubber flows easily. As the rubber gradually dries out, increase the pressure.

Never bring the pad to rest on the surface of the polish. As you reach the edge of the workpiece, sweep the rubber off the surface and sweep it back on again for the next pass. If you pull the

Woodwork must be prepared immaculately before polishing, as every blemish will be mirrored in the finish. The grain should be filled, either with a proprietary filler ($\triangleright$) or by layers of polish, which are rubbed down and repeated until the pores of the wood are filled flush with polish.

Work in a warm, dust-free room:

rubber off the workpiece it will leave a blemish in the polish.

Cover the surface, perhaps ten or twelve times. As you feel the rubber drying out, open it up and pour a little more shellac onto the back of the cotton wool filling. Occasionally change the rag for a spare one, leaving the used one to soak in a jar of methylated spirit to wash out the polish ready for the next exchange.

Seal the rubber in an empty glass jar and leave the surface to harden for about one hour, then if necessary, lightly flatten the polish with silicon carbide paper using fingertip pressure.

Build up another layer of polish with the rubber. Vary the size and shape of your strokes so that every part of the surface is covered (see below). In between each coat, make straight parallel strokes along the grain.

Repeat the process for a third time, more if you want a deeper colour. Make your final coat with slightly less polish; allow it to harden overnight.

Burnishing the polished surface

Take a handful of clean cotton wool and dampen the sole with burnishing liquid. Use it to burnish a small section at a time, rubbing forcefully along the grain. As the sole of the pad becomes dirty, pull it off to reveal a clean surface. Buff each section with a soft duster before burnishing the next.

dust's effect is obvious, but a low temperature will make the polish go cloudy (bloom).

Work in a good light so that you can glance across the surface to gauge the quality of the finish you are applying.

TRADITIONAL FRENCH POLISHING

With traditional polishing, the shellac is thicker therefore do not soak the rag with meths. Charge the rubber and dab linseed oil on the sole.

Apply all the shellac with a rubber, using a combination of strokes (see below). Recharge the rubber and add a touch of oil to the sole when it starts to drag or catch. Leave to dry for twenty minutes. Repeat four or five times.

Leave to harden overnight then build up more layers – ten may be enough but continue until you're happy with the depth of colour. To remove surface marks, rub down the hard polish with silicon carbide paper. The top layer may be streaked due to the linseed oil: add meths to the rubber's cotton wool. Burnish with straight strokes parallel with the grain, sweeping the rubber on and off at each end. As the rubber drags, recharge. Leave for a few minutes to see if the streaking disappears. If not, repeat with more meths. Polish with a duster and leave to harden.

Apply French polish with a rubber

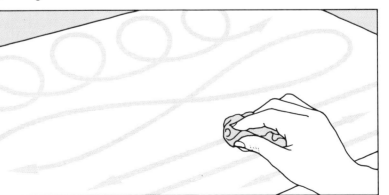

Using the rubber
Apply the polish with a combination of circular and figure-of-eight strokes so that every part of the surface is covered. When you finish each coat, run the rubber in long straight strokes, parallel to the wood grain. Keep the pad moving constantly and smoothly: if you lift it from the surface a scar will form.

Making a rubber for basic polishing
Saturate a 300mm (1ft) square of white cotton rag with meths, wring out until damp, dip a handful of cotton wool into the shellac and squeeze out excess. Wrap in rag, twist excess into a handgrip; smooth sole of rubber.

COLD CURE LACQUER

Due to its chemical composition, careful preparation is essential or plastic coating will take days to cure instead of only two hours. It must be applied to a clean, grease-free surface, which has been sanded smooth. Strip the old finish but do not use a caustic stripper, as this will react against the coating.

Clean old wax polish from the wood. You must remove every trace, even from the pores of the timber. Wash it with white spirit, using a ball of fine wire wool in the direction of the grain. When the wood is dry, scrub it with water and detergent, then rinse the surface with clean water with a little white vinegar added.

If you use wood stain, make sure it is made by the manufacturer of the lacquer, otherwise it might change colour. Use the same manufacturer's stopping to fill cracks and holes and never use plaster or plastic fillers.

Mixing cold cure lacquer

In most cases, it's best to use a paintbrush to apply plastic coating, although you can use a plastic foam roller instead, especially for large areas of woodwork.

When you are ready to apply the lacquer, mix the coating and hardener in a glass, polythene or enamel container.

Use the proportions recommended by the manufacturer. Mix just enough for your immediate needs, as it will set in two to three days in an open dish. Don't be tempted to economize by pouring mixed lacquer back into its original container: the hardener will ruin any remaining substance.

Applying the lacquer

Plastic coating must be applied in a warm atmosphere. Use a well-loaded applicator and spread the lacquer onto the wood. There is no need to over-brush the liquid as it will flow unaided and even a thick coat will cure thoroughly and smoothly. Plastic coating dries quickly and will begin to show brush marks if disturbed after 10 to 15 minutes, so you should work swiftly to pick up the wet edges.

After two hours, apply the second coat. If necessary, rub down the hardened lacquer with fine abrasive paper to remove blemishes, then add a third coat. You will achieve better adhesion between the layers if you can apply all the coats in one day, so long as each has time to dry.

Burnishing lacquer

If you want a mirror finish, wait for 24 hours then use a proprietary burnishing cream. Rub down the lacquer with very fine abrasive paper or wire wool, then rub the cream onto the surface with a soft cloth. Burnish it vigorously with a clean soft duster to achieve the required depth of sheen.

Matting lacquer

To produce a subtle satin coat, rub the hardened lacquer along the grain with fine wire wool dipped in wax polish. The grade of the wire wool will effect the degree of matting. Use very fine 000 grade for a satin finish and a coarse 0 grade for a fully-matted surface. Polish with a clean, soft duster.

● **Spontaneous combustion**
It is essential to dispose of oily rags immediately you have finished with them as they have been known to burst into flames.

SAFETY WHEN USING LACQUER

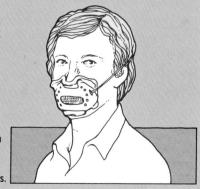

Although cold cure lacquer is safe to use, you should take care when applying it to a large surface such as a floor, due to the concentration of fumes.

Open all windows and doors if possible for ventilation – but remember the necessity for a warm atmosphere, too – and take the extra precaution of wearing a simple gauze facemask to prevent you breathing in the fumes. You can buy cheap masks and spare lint filters, which you should renew frequently, from chemists and DIY stores.

OILING AND WAXING WOODWORK

Applying the oil

Clean and prepare the wood for oiling. Remove previous finishes carefully so that oil can penetrate the grain.

The most efficient way to apply a finishing oil is to rub it into the wood with a soft, lint-free rag in the form of a rubber (◁). Don't store oily rags: keep them in a sealed tin while the job is in progress then unfold them and leave them outside to dry before throwing them away.

A brush is a convenient way to spread oil liberally over large surfaces and into carvings or deep mouldings.

Rub or brush a generous coating of oil into the wood grain. Leave it to soak in for a few minutes, then rub off excess oil with a clean cloth. After about six hours, coat the wood with oil once more. The next day, apply a third and final coat; raise a faint sheen by burnishing with a soft duster.

Wax polishing timber

If you want to wax-polish new timber, seal the wood first with one coat of clear varnish (or French polish on fine furniture). This will stop the wax being absorbed too deeply into the wood and provides a slightly more durable finish. Before waxing an old clear finish, clean it first to remove deposits of dirt and possibly an old wax dressing.

To remove dirty wax, mix up white spirit with 25 per cent linseed oil. Use the liquid to clean the surface quite hard with a coarse cloth. If there is no obvious improvement, try dipping very fine wire wool into the cleaner and rub in the direction of the grain. Don't press too hard as you want to remove wax and dirt only without damaging the finish below. Wash the cleaned surface with a cloth dipped in white spirit and leave to dry before refinishing.

You can use a soft cloth to apply wax polish but use a paintbrush to spread liquid wax over a wide area. Pour liquid wax polish onto a cloth pad and rub it into the sealed wood with a circular motion followed by strokes parallel with the grain. Make this first coat a generous one.

Buff up the wax after one hour then apply a second, thinner coat in the direction of the grain only. Burnish this coat lightly and leave it for several hours to harden. Bring the surface to a high gloss by burnishing vigorously with a soft duster.

FINISHING METALWORK

Ferrous metals that are rusty will shed any paint film rapidly, so the most important aspect of finishing metalwork is thorough preparation and priming to prevent this corrosion from returning; then applying the finish is virtually the same as painting woodwork.

When you are choosing a finish for metalwork in and around the house (see chart below and table overleaf for suitable types) make sure it fulfils your requirements. Many of the finishes listed are easy to apply to metal, but the ability of some to withstand heavy wear is likely to be poor (▷)

Methods of application

Most of the finishes suggested for use on metalwork can be applied with a paintbrush. The exception is black lead (▷). In the main, use the standard techniques for painting woodwork (▷), but bitumen-based paints should be laid on only and not brushed out like conventional coatings.

Remove metal door and window fittings for painting, suspending them on wire hooks to dry. Make sure that sharp or hard edges are coated properly, as

the finish can wear thin quickly.

Some paints can be sprayed but there are few situations where it is advantageous, except perhaps for intricately moulded ironwork such as garden furniture, which you can paint outside – otherwise ventilation is a necessity indoors.

A roller is suitable on large flat surfaces and pipework requires its own special V-section roller (▷), which is designed to coat curved surfaces.

● Black dot denotes compatibility. Thorough preparation is essential before applying any finish to metals (▷).

FINISHES FOR METALWORK

	Oil paint	Emulsion paint	Metallic paint	Bituminous based paint	Security paint	Radiator enamel	Black lead	Varnish	Bath paint	Non-slip paint
DRYING TIME: HOURS										
Touch-dry	4	1-2	4	1-2		2-6		0-3	6-10	4-6
Re-coatable	14	4	8	6-24		7-14		1	16-24	12
THINNERS: SOLVENTS										
Water		●			●					
White spirit	●		●	●	●		●	●	●	●
Special						●				
Cellulose thinners								●		
NUMBER OF COATS										
Normal conditions	1-2	2	1-2	1-3	1	1-2	VARIABLE	1-2	2	2
COVERAGE										
Sq metres per litre	12-16	9-15	10-14	6-15	2½	13	VARIABLE	13	13-14	3-5
METHOD OF APPLICATION										
Brush	●	●	●	●	●	●	●	●	●	●
Roller	●	●	●							
Spray gun	●	●	●					●		
Cloth pad (Rubber)							●			

PAINTING RADIATORS AND PIPES

Leave radiators and hot water pipes to cool before you paint them. The only problem with decorating a radiator is how to paint the back: the best solution is to remove it completely or, if possible, swing it away from the wall, paint the back, reposition the radiator then paint the front.

If this is inconvenient, use a special radiator brush with a long metal handle (see right). Use the same tool to paint in between the leaves of a double radiator. It is difficult to achieve a perfect finish even with the brush, so aim at covering

areas you are likely to see when the radiator is fixed in position rather than a complete application.

Don't paint over radiator valves or fittings or you will not be able to operate them afterwards.

Paint pipework lengthwise rather than across, or runs are likely to form. The first coat on metal piping will be streaky, so be prepared to apply two or three coats. Unless you are using radiator enamel, allow the paint to harden thoroughly before turning on the heat, or it may blister.

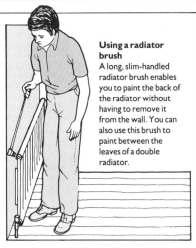

Using a radiator brush
A long, slim-handled radiator brush enables you to paint the back of the radiator without having to remove it from the wall. You can also use this brush to paint between the leaves of a double radiator.

METALWORK

SUITABLE FINISHES FOR METALWORK

Gutters and downpipes

It is best to coat the inside of gutters with a bituminous paint for thorough protection against moisture, but you can finish the outer surfaces with oil paint or security paint.

To protect the wall behind a downpipe, slip a scrap of card between while painting the back of the pipe (1).

Metal casement windows

Paint metal casement windows using the sequence described for wooden casements (◁), which allows you to close the frame at night without spoiling a freshly-painted surface.

Varnishing metalwork

Polish the metal to a high gloss then use a nail brush to scrub it with warm water containing some liquid detergent. Rinse the metal in clean water then dry it thoroughly with an absorbent cloth.

Use a large, soft artist's brush to paint on acrylic lacquer (2), working swiftly from the top. Let the lacquer flow naturally, working all round the object to keep the wet edge moving.

If you do leave a brush stroke in partially-set varnish, do not try to overpaint it but finish the job then warm the metal (by standing it on a radiator if possible). As soon as the blemish disappears, remove the object from the heat and allow it to cool gradually in a dust-free atmosphere.

Blacking cast iron

Black lead produces an attractive finish for cast iron. It is not a permanent or durable finish and will have to be renewed periodically. It may transfer if rubbed hard.

The material is supplied in a toothpaste-like tube. Squeeze some of the black cream onto a soft cloth and spread it onto the metal. Use an old toothbrush (3) to scrub it into decorative ironwork for best coverage.

When you have covered the surface, buff the black lead to a satin sheen with a clean, dry cloth. Build up a patina with several applications of black lead for a moisture-proof finish.

1 Protect wall
Use card behind a downpipe when painting behind it.

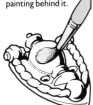

2 Apply lacquer
Use a large, soft artist's paintbrush.

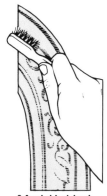

3 Apply black lead
Scrub cream into intricate surfaces using an old toothbrush.

Standard oil paints are perfectly suitable for metal. Having primed the surface, interior metalwork will need at least one undercoat plus a top coat. Add an extra undercoat for greater protection of exterior metalwork.

EMULSION PAINT

Strictly, emulsion paint is not suitable for finishing metal. Being water-based, it may promote corrosion on ferrous metals if applied directly; it can be used to paint radiators to match the wall colour if the metal has been factory-painted.

METALLIC PAINT

For a metallic-like finish, choose a paint containing aluminium, copper, gold or bronze powders: these paints are water-resistant and are able to withstand very high temperatures – up to about 100°C (212° F).

BITUMINOUS PAINT

Bitumen-based paints give economical protection for exterior storage tanks and piping. Standard bituminous paint is black but there is also a limited range of colours, plus 'modified' bituminous paint, which contains aluminium.

Before coating the inside of drinking water tanks, make sure the paint is non-contaminating. Don't apply over other types of paint.

SECURITY PAINT

Non-setting security paint, primarily for rainwater and waste downpipes, remains slippery to prevent intruders from scaling the wall via the pipe. Restrict it to pipework over about 1.8m (6ft) above the ground, out of reach.

RADIATOR ENAMEL

A heat-stoving acrylic paint which is applied in two thin coats. It can be used over emulsion or oil paints so long as these have not been recently applied (don't rub them down first).

Apply a compatible metal primer over new paint or factory priming to prevent strong solvents in the enamel reacting with the previous coating. A special thinner is required for brush cleaning. A choice of satin and gloss finishes is available.

Finish the radiator in position then turn the heating on (boiler set to maximum) for a minimum of two hours to bake the enamel onto the metal. Apply a second coat six to eight hours later.

Also use to repaint central heating boiler cabinets, refrigerators, cookers and washing machines.

BLACK LEAD

A cream used to colour cast ironwork, it is a mixture of graphite and waxes. After several coats it is moisture-proof, but it is not suitable for exterior use.

VARNISHES

Virtually any clear lacquer can be used on polished metalwork without spoiling its appearance, but many polyurethanes yellow with age. An acrylic lacquer is clear and will protect chrome-plating, brass and copper – even outside.

NON-SLIP PAINT

Designed to provide good foot-holding on a wide range of surfaces, including metal, non-slip paint is ideal for painting metal spiral staircase treads and exterior fire escapes. The surface must be primed before application.

APPLYING TEXTURED COATING

You can apply the coating with either a roller or a broad wall brush: finer textures are possible using the latter. Buy a special roller if recommended by the coating manufacturer.

With a well-loaded roller, apply a generous coat in a 600mm (2ft) wide band across the ceiling or down a wall. Do not press too hard and vary the angle of the stroke.

If you decide to brush on the coating, do not spread it out like paint. Lay it on with one stroke and spread it back again with one or two strokes only.

Clean up any splashes then apply a second band and texture it, blending both bands together. Continue in this way until the wall or ceiling is complete. Keep the room ventilated until the coating has hardened.

Painting around fittings
Use a small paintbrush to fill in around electrical fittings and along edges, trying to copy the texture used on the surrounding wall or ceiling. Some people prefer to form a distinct margin around fittings by drawing a small paintbrush along the perimeter to give a smooth finish.

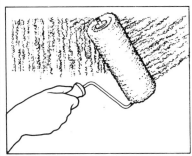

Creating a texture
You can experiment with a variety of tools to make any number of textures. You can use a standard roller, or use ones made with special surfaces to produce diagonal or diamond patterns, or you can apply a swirling, ripple or stipple finish with improvized equipment, as shown right.

TEXTURED COATINGS

Textured coatings can be obtained as a dry powder for mixing with warm water, or in a ready-mixed form for direct application from the tub. Most manufacturers supply a fine or a thick mix; if you want a heavy texture, choose the thicker mix. Where you're likely to rub against the wall – in a narrow hall, small bathroom or

children's room, a fine texture is preferable: the coating dries very hard and could graze your skin.

Textured coatings are suitable for exterior walls as well as indoors. They are also available in a range of colours – you can cover the texture with emulsion paint if a standard colour does not fit your decorative scheme.

Preparing for textured coatings

New surfaces will need virtually no preparation, but joints between plasterboard must be reinforced with tape. Strip any old wallcoverings and key gloss paint with glasspaper. Old walls and ceilings must be clean, dry, sound and free from organic growth. Treat friable surfaces with stabilizing solution (▷).

Although large cracks and holes must be filled, a textured coating will conceal minor defects in walls and ceilings by filling small cracks and bridging shallow bumps and hollows.

Masking joinery and fittings
Use 50mm (2in) wide masking tape to cover door and window frames, electrical socket outlets, switches and ceiling roses, plumbing pipework, picture rails and skirting boards. Lay dust sheets over the floor.

I Diamond pattern

2 Stipple effect

3 Swirl design

4 Combed arcs

5 Tree bark simulation

6 Stucco finish

I Geometric patterns
Use a roller with diamond or diagonal grooves: load the roller and draw lightly across the textured surface.

2 Stippled finish
Pat the coating with a damp sponge to create a pitted profile. Rinse out frequently. Alter your wrist angle and overlap sections.

3 Random swirls
Twist a damp sponge on the textured surface, then pull away to make a swirling design. Overlap swirls for a layered effect.

4 Combed arcs
A toothed spatula sold with the finish is used to create combed patterns: arcs, criss-cross patterns or wavy scrolls.

5 Imitation tree bark
Produce a bark texture by applying parallel strokes with a roller then lightly drawing the straight edge of a spatula over it.

6 Stucco finish
Apply parallel roller strokes, then run the rounded corner of a spatula over it in short straight strokes.

49

WALLCOVERINGS

Although wallcoverings are often called 'wallpaper', only a proportion of the wide range available is made solely from wood pulp. There is a huge range of paper-backed fabrics from exotic silks to coarse hessians; other types include natural textures such as cork or woven grass on a paper backing. Plastics have widened the choice of wallcoverings still further: there are paper- or cotton-backed vinyls, and plain or patterned foamed plastics. Before wallpaper became popular, fabric wall hangings were used to decorate interiors and this is still possible today, using unbacked fabrics glued or stretched across walls.

Top right
1 Expanded polystyrene
2 Lining paper
3 Woodchip

Bottom left
4 Hand-printed
5 Machine-printed

Bottom right
6 Anaglypta
7 Supaglypta
8 Lincrustas
9 Vinaglypta

Ensuring a suitable surface

Although many wallcoverings will cover minor blemishes, walls and ceilings should be clean, sound and smooth. Eradicate damp and organic growth before hanging any wallcovering. Consider whether you should size the walls to reduce paste absorption (◁).

COVERINGS THAT CAMOUFLAGE

Although a poor surface should be repaired, some coverings hide minor blemishes as well as providing a foundation for other finishes.

Expanded polystyrene sheet
Thin polystyrene sheet is used for lining a wall before papering. It reduces condensation but will also bridge hairline cracks and small holes. Polystyrene dents easily, so don't use where it will take a lot of punishment. A patterned ceiling version is made.

Lining paper
A cheap, buff coloured wallpaper for lining uneven or impervious walls prior to hanging a heavy or expensive wallcovering. Can also provide an even surface for emulsion paint.

Woodchip paper
Woodchip or ingrain paper is a relief covering made by sandwiching particles of wood between two layers of paper. It's inexpensive, easy to hang (but a problem to cut), and must be painted.

Relief papers ▷
'Whites', or relief papers, with a deeply embossed pattern, are for hiding minor imperfections and for over-painting.

Anaglypta is made by bonding two sheets of paper together, which then pass between embossing rollers. A stronger version, *Supaglypta,* is made using cotton fibres instead of wood pulp, and withstands deeper embossing.

The raised pattern on *Lincrusta* is a solid film of linseed oil and fillers fused onto a backing paper before the pattern is applied by an engraved steel roller. Deep relief wallcoverings are made from vinyl – notably *Vinaglypta* – either as solid plastic, or it is heated in an oven, which 'blows' or expands the vinyl, embossing it. Relief vinyls are intended to be painted over.

◁ Printed wallpapers
One advantage of ordinary wallpaper is the superb range of printed colours and patterns, which is much wider than for any other covering. Most papers – the cheapest – are machine-printed.

Hand-printed papers are more costly. Inks have a tendency to run if you smear paste on the surface, are prone to tearing when wet, and are not really suitable for walls exposed to wear or condensation. Pattern matching can be awkward, because hand-printing isn't as accurate as machine printing.

WALLCOVERINGS

Washable papers
Ordinary printed papers with a thin, impervious glaze of PVA to make a spongeable surface, washables are suitable for bathrooms and kitchens. The surface must not be scrubbed or the plastic coating will be worn away.

Vinyl wallcoverings
A base paper, or sometimes a cotton backing, is coated with a layer of vinyl upon which the design is printed. Heat is used to fuse the colours and vinyl. The result is a durable, washable wallcovering ideally suited to bathrooms and kitchens. Many vinyls are sold ready-pasted for easy application.

Foamed polyethylene coverings
A lightweight wallcovering, called *Novamura,* made solely of foamed plastic with no backing paper. It is printed with a wide range of patterns, colours and designs. You paste the wall instead of the covering. It is best used on walls that are not exposed to wear.

Flock wallcoverings
Flock papers have the major pattern elements picked out with a fine pile produced by gluing synthetic or natural fibres (such as silk or wool) to the backing paper, so that it stands out in relief, with a velvet-like texture.
　　Standard flocks are difficult to hang as paste will ruin the pile. Vinyl flocks are less delicate, can be hung anywhere, and may even be ready-pasted.
　　You can sponge flock paper to remove stains, but brush to remove dust from the pile. Vinyl flocks can be washed without risk of damage.

Foil wallcoverings
Paper-backed foils are coated with a metallized plastic film to give a shiny finish. They are expensive but come in a range of beautiful contrasting textures (over-printed designs allow the foil to show through). Foils should not be used on uneven walls, as the shine will highlight imperfections.

Glass fibre wallcovering
Woven glass fibre fabric is a durable fire-resistant wallcovering that will bridge minor irregularities. After 24 hours, the fabric can be painted.

Grass cloth
Natural grasses are woven into a mat, which is glued to a paper backing. These wallcoverings are very attractive but fragile and difficult to hang.

Cork-faced paper
A wallpaper surfaced with thin sheets of coloured or natural cork, which is not as easily spoiled as other special papers.

Paper-backed fabrics
Finely woven cotton, linen or silk on a paper backing must be applied to a flat surface. They are expensive, not easy to hang, and you must avoid smearing the fabric with adhesive. Most fabrics are delicate but some are plastic-coated to make them scuff-resistant.

Unbacked fabrics
Upholstery width fabric – typically hessian – can be wrapped around panels, glued to the wall.

SEE ALSO

Details for: ▷	
Sizing walls	22
Choosing colour/pattern	6–7, 11
Preparing plaster	22–23
Mould growth	24
Stripping wallpaper	24

Left to right
1 Washable papers
2 Vinyls
3 Foamed polyethylene
4 Flock papers
5 Foil papers
6 Glass fibre
7 Cork faced papers
8 Paper-backed fabrics
9 Unbacked fabrics
10 Grass cloth mats

WALLCOVERINGS: ESTIMATING QUANTITIES

Calculating the number of rolls of wallcovering you will need to cover your walls and ceiling depends on the size of the roll – both length and width – the pattern repeat and the obstructions you have to avoid. Because of variations in colour between batches, you must take into account all these points – and allow for wastage, too. A standard roll of wallcovering measures 530mm (1ft 9in) wide and 10.05 metres (33ft) long. Use the two charts on this page to estimate how many rolls you will need for walls and ceilings.

SEE ALSO

◁ Details for:
Wallcoverings 50–51
Papering walls 54–57
Papering ceilings 58

Estimating non-standard rolls

If the wallcovering is not cut to a standard size, calculate the amount you need in this way:

Walls

Measure the height of the walls from skirting to ceiling. Divide the length of the roll by this figure to find the number of wall lengths you can cut from a roll.

Measure around the room, excluding windows and doors, to work out how many widths fit into the total length of the walls. Divide this number by the number of wall lengths you can get from one roll to find how many rolls you need.

Make an allowance for short lengths above doors and under windows.

Ceilings

Measure the length of the room to determine one strip of paper. Work out how many roll widths fit across the room. Multiply the two figures. Divide the answer by the length of a roll to find out how many rolls you need. Check for waste and allow for it.

Checking for shading

If rolls of wallcovering are printed in one batch, there should be no problem with colour matching one roll to another. When you buy, look for the batch number printed on the wrapping.

Make a visual check before hanging the covering, especially for hand-printed papers or fabrics. Unroll a short length of each roll and lay them side by side. You may get a better colour match by changing the rolls around, but if colour difference is obvious, ask for a replacement roll.

Some wallcoverings are marked 'reverse alternate lengths' in order to even out any colour variations. Take this into account when checking.

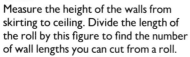

Measuring walls for standard rolls
You can include windows and doors in your estimate.

Measuring walls for non-standard rolls
Do not include doors and windows when estimating for expensive materials. Allow for short lengths afterwards.

Walls: Standard rolls
Measure your room, then look down height column and across wall column to assess number of standard rolls required.

WALLS	HEIGHT OF ROOM IN METRES FROM SKIRTING							
MEASUREMENT IN METRES AROUND WALLS INCLUDING DOORS AND WINDOWS	2.0-2.25m	2.25-2.50m	2.50-2.75m	2.75-3.0m	3.0-3.25m	3.25-3.50m	3.50-3.75m	3.75-4.0m
	NUMBER OF ROLLS REQUIRED FOR WALLS							
10.0m	5	5	6	6	7	7	8	8
10.5m	5	6	6	7	7	8	8	9
11.0m	5	6	7	7	8	8	9	9
11.5m	6	6	7	7	8	8	9	9
12.0m	6	6	7	8	8	9	9	10
12.5m	6	7	7	8	9	9	10	10
13.0m	6	7	8	8	9	10	10	10
13.5m	7	7	8	9	9	10	10	11
14.0m	7	7	8	9	10	10	11	11
14.5m	7	8	8	9	10	10	11	12
15.0m	7	8	9	9	10	11	12	12
15.5m	7	8	9	9	10	11	12	13
16.0m	8	8	9	10	11	11	12	13
16.5m	8	9	9	10	11	12	13	13
17.0m	8	9	10	10	11	12	13	14
17.5m	8	9	10	11	12	13	14	14
18.0m	9	9	10	11	12	13	14	15
18.5m	9	10	11	12	12	13	14	15
19.0m	9	10	11	12	13	14	15	16
19.5m	9	10	11	12	13	14	15	16
20.0m	9	10	11	12	13	14	15	16
20.5m	10	11	12	13	14	15	16	17
21.0m	10	11	12	13	14	15	16	17
21.5m	10	11	12	13	14	15	17	18
22.0m	10	11	13	14	15	16	17	18
22.5m	11	12	13	14	15	16	17	18
23.0m	11	12	13	14	15	17	18	19
23.5m	11	12	13	15	16	17	18	19
24.0m	11	12	14	15	16	17	18	20
24.5m	11	13	14	15	16	18	19	20
25.0m	12	13	14	15	17	18	19	20
25.5m	12	13	14	16	17	18	20	21
26.0m	12	13	15	16	17	19	20	21
26.5m	12	14	15	16	18	19	20	22
27.0m	13	14	15	17	18	19	21	22
27.5m	13	14	16	17	18	20	21	23
28.0m	13	14	16	17	19	20	21	23
28.5m	13	15	16	18	19	20	22	23
29.0m	13	15	16	18	19	21	22	24
29.5m	14	15	17	18	20	21	23	24
30.0m	14	15	17	18	20	21	23	24

Ceilings: Standard rolls
Number of standard rolls required are shown next to overall room dimensions.

Dimensions
All dimensions are shown in metres.
(1m = 39in)

CEILINGS: NUMBER OF ROLLS REQUIRED							
Measurement around room (m)	Number of rolls	Measurement around room (m)	Number of rolls	Measurement around room (m)	Number of rolls	Measurement around room (m)	Number of rolls
11.0	2	16.0	4	21.0	6	26.0	9
12.0	2	17.0	4	22.0	7	27.0	10
13.0	3	18.0	5	23.0	7	28.0	10
14.0	3	19.0	5	24.0	8	29.0	11
15.0	4	20.0	5	25.0	8	30.0	11

TRIMMING AND CUTTING TECHNIQUES

Most wallcoverings are already machine-trimmed to width so that you can butt-join adjacent lengths accurately. Some hand-printed papers and speciality coverings are left untrimmed. These are usually expensive, so don't attempt to trim them yourself: ask the supplier to do this for you – it's worth the slight additional cost.

Cutting plain wallcoverings

To cut a plain paper to length, measure the height of the wall at the point where you will hang the first 'drop'. Add an extra 100mm (4in) for trimming top and bottom. Cut several pieces from your first roll to the same length and mark the top of each one.

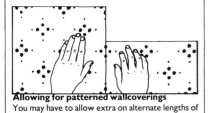

Allowing for patterned wallcoverings
You may have to allow extra on alternate lengths of patterned wallcoverings to match patterns. Check before you cut your second length.

CHOOSING PASTE

Most wallpaper pastes are supplied as powder or flakes for mixing with water. There are several specific types:

All-purpose paste
Standard wallpaper paste is suitable for most light- to medium-weight papers. By adding less water, it can be used to hang heavyweight papers.

Heavy-duty paste
Specially prepared to hang embossed papers, paper-backed fabrics and other heavyweight wallcoverings.

Fungicidal paste
Most pastes contain a fungicide to prevent mould growth under certain impervious wallcoverings, which slow down the drying rate of the paste. It is essential to use a fungicidal paste when hanging vinyls, washable papers, foils and foamed plastic coverings.

Ready-mixed paste
Tubs of ready-mixed, thixotropic paste are specially made to give the high adhesion required for heavyweight luxury wallcoverings such as fabric.

PASTING WALLCOVERINGS

You can use any wipe-clean table for pasting, but a narrow fold-up pasting table is a good investment if you are doing a lot of decorating. Lay several cut lengths of paper on top of each other face down on the table to keep it clean. Tuck the ends under a length of string tied loosely round the table legs to stop the paper rolling up while you paste it.

Applying the paste

Use a large, soft wall brush or pasting brush to apply the paste. Mix the paste in a plastic bucket and tie string across the rim to support the brush, keeping its handle clean while you paperhang.

Align the covering with the far edge of the table (so you don't get paste on the table, then transfer it to the face of the wall covering). Apply the paste by brushing away from the centre. Paste the edges and remove any lumps.

If you prefer, apply the paste with a short-piled paint roller; pour the paste into a roller tray. Roll in one direction only towards the end of the paper.

Pull the covering to the front edge of the table and paste the other half. Fold the pasted end over – don't press it down – and slide the length along the table to expose an unpasted part.

Paste the other end then fold it over to almost meet the first cut end: the second fold is invariably deeper than the first, a good way to denote the bottom of patterned wallcoverings. Fold long drops concertina-fashion.

Leave the pasted covering to soak, draped over a broom handle spanning two chair backs. Some heavy or embossed coverings may need to soak for 15 minutes: let one length soak while you hang another. Vinyls and lightweight papers can be hung immediately.

Pasting the wall

Hang exotic wallcoverings by pasting the wall, to reduce the risk of marking their delicate faces. Apply a band of paste just wider than the length of covering, so that you will not have to paste right up to its edge for the next length. Use a brush or roller.

Ready-pasted wallcoverings

Many wallcoverings come pre-coated with adhesive, activated by soaking a cut length in a trough of cold water (▷). Mix ordinary paste to recoat dry edges.

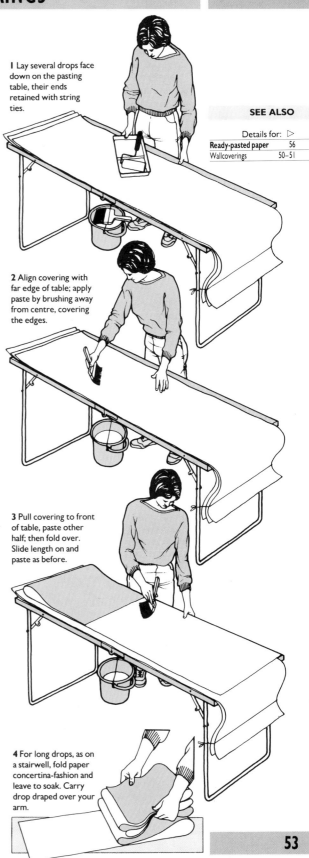

1 Lay several drops face down on the pasting table, their ends retained with string ties.

SEE ALSO
Details for: ▷
Ready-pasted paper 56
Wallcoverings 50–51

2 Align covering with far edge of table; apply paste by brushing away from centre, covering the edges.

3 Pull covering to front of table, paste other half; then fold over. Slide length on and paste as before.

4 For long drops, as on a stairwell, fold paper concertina-fashion and leave to soak. Carry drop draped over your arm.

● **Hide a join in a corner**
When you are using a wallcovering with a large pattern, try to finish in a corner where you will not notice if the pattern does not match.

Sticking down the edges
Ensure that the edges of the paper adhere firmly by running a seam roller along the butt join.

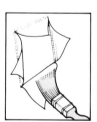

Losing air bubbles
Slight blistering usually flattens out as wet paper dries and shrinks slightly. If you find that a blister remains, either inject a little paste through it and roll it flat, or cut across it in two directions, peel back the triangular flaps and paste them down.

LINING A WALL

Lining a wall prior to decorating is only necessary if you are hanging embossed or luxury wallcoverings, or if the wall is uneven and imperfections might show through a thin paper. Lining paper is hung horizontally so that the joins cannot align with those in the top layer. Work from right to left if you are right-handed, vice versa if you are left-handed.

Mark a horizontal line near the top of the wall, one roll width from the ceiling. Holding the concertina-folded length in one hand, start at the top right-hand corner of the wall, aligning the bottom edge with the marked line. Smooth the paper onto the wall with a paperhanger's brush, working from the centre towards the edges.

Work along the wall gradually, unfolding the length as you do so. Take care not to stretch or tear the wet paper. Use the brush to gently stipple the edge into the corner at each end.

Use the point of a pair of scissors to lightly mark the corner, peel back the paper and trim to the line. Brush the paper back in place. You may have to perform a similar operation along the ceiling if the paper overlaps slightly. Work down the wall butting each strip against the last, or leave a tiny gap between the lengths.

Trim the bottom length to the skirting. Leave the lining paper to dry out for 24 hours before covering.

Lining prior to painting
If you line a wall for emulsion painting, hang the paper vertically as for other wallcoverings as the joins will be minimally visible.

Hanging lining paper horizontally
Hold the concertina-folded paper in one hand and smooth onto the wall from top right, butting strips.

PAPERING A WALL

Where to start

Don't apply wallcovering until all the woodwork has been painted or varnished (◁) and start by painting or papering the ceiling (◁).

The traditional method for papering a room is to hang the first length next to a window close to a corner, then work in both directions away from the light, but you may find it easier to paper the longest uninterrupted wall to get used to the basic techniques before tackling corners or obstructions.

If your wallcovering has a large regular motif, centre the first length over the fireplace for symmetry. You could centre this first length between two windows, unless you will be left with narrow strips each side, in which case it's best to butt two lengths on the centre line.

Centre a large motif over fireplace

Or butt two lengths between windows

Hanging on a straight wall

The walls of an average room are rarely truly square, so use a plumb line to mark a vertical guide against which to set the first length of wallcovering. Start at one end of the wall and mark the vertical line one roll width away from the corner, minus 12mm (½in) so the first length will overlap the adjacent wall.

Allowing enough wallcovering for trimming at the ceiling, unfold the top section of the pasted length and hold it against the plumbed line. Using a paperhanger's brush, work gently out from the centre in all directions to squeeze out any trapped air.

When you are sure the paper is positioned accurately, mark the ceiling line with outer edge of your scissors blade, peel back the top edge and cut along the crease. Smooth the paper back and stipple it down carefully with the brush. Unpeel the lower fold of the paper, smooth it onto the wall with the brush then stipple it firmly into the corner. Trim the bottom edge against the skirting, peel away, trim and brush back against the wall.

Hang the next length in the same way. Slide it with your fingertips to align the pattern and produce a perfect butt joint. Wipe any paste from the surface with a damp cloth. Continue to the other side of the wall, allowing the last drop to overlap the adjoining wall by 12mm (½in).

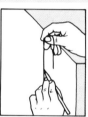

1 Mark first length
Use a roll of paper to mark the wall one width away from the corner – less 12mm (½in) for an overlap onto the return wall – then draw a line from ceiling to skirting using a plumb line.

2 Hang first drop
Cut the first drop of paper, allowing about 50mm (2in) at each end for trimming, paste and allow to soak. Hang the top fold against the plumbed line and brush out from the centre, working down.

3 Trim at ceiling
When the paper is smoothly brushed on, run the outer edge of your scissors along the ceiling angle, peel away the paper, cut off the excess then brush back onto the wall.

4 Trim at skirting
Hang the lower fold of paper. At the skirting, tap your brush gently into the top edge, peel away the paper and cut along the folded line with scissors, then brush back.

PAPERING PROBLEM AREAS

Papering around doors and windows

Hang the length next to a door frame, brushing down the butt joint to align the pattern, but allow the other edge to loosely overlap the door.

Make a diagonal cut in the excess towards the top corner of the frame (**1**). Crease the waste along the frame with scissors, peel it back, trim it off then brush it back. Leave a 12mm (½in) strip for turning onto the top of the frame. Fill in over the door.

Butt the next full length over the door and cut the excess diagonally into the frame so that you can paste the rest of the strip down the side of the door. Mark and cut off the waste.

When papering up to flush window frames, treat them like a door. Where a window is set into a reveal, hang the length of wallcovering next to the window and allow it to overhang the opening. Make a horizontal cut just above the edge of the window reveal. Make a similar cut near the bottom then fold the paper around to cover the side of the reveal. Crease and trim along the window frame and sill.

Cut a strip of paper to match the width and pattern of the overhang above the window reveal. Paste it, slip it under the overhang and fold it around the top of the reveal (**2**). Cut through the overlap with a smooth, wavy stroke, remove the excess paper and roll down the join (**3**).

To continue, hang short lengths on the wall below and above the window, wrapping top lengths into the reveal.

1 Cut the overlap diagonally into the frame

Papering around a fireplace

Paper around a fireplace as for a door. Make a diagonal cut in the waste overlapping the fireplace, up to the edge of the mantel shelf, so that you can tuck the paper in all round for creasing and trimming to the surround.

To cut to an ornate surround, paper the wall above the surround; cut strips to fit under the mantel at each side, turning them around the corners of the chimney breast. Gently press the wallcovering into the moulding, peel it away and cut round the impression using nail scissors. Brush the paper back.

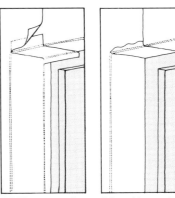

2 Fold onto reveal top   **3 Cut with wavy line**

Papering internal and external corners

Turn an internal corner by marking another plumbed line so that the next length of paper covers the overlap from the first wall. If the piece you trimmed off at the corner is wide enough, use it as your first length on the new wall.

To turn an external corner, trim the last length so that it wraps around it, lapping the next wall by about 25mm (1in). Plumb and hang the remaining strip with its edge about 12mm (½in) from the corner.

Internal corner

12mm (½in) overlap ▷

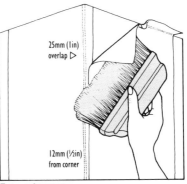

25mm (1in) overlap ▷

12mm (½in) from corner

External corner

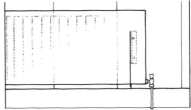

Slit to top of bracket behind radiator

Papering behind radiators

If you can't remove a radiator, turn off the heating and allow it to cool. Use a steel tape to measure the positions of the brackets holding the radiator to the wall. Transfer these measurements to a length of wallcovering, slit it from the bottom up to the top of the bracket. Feed the pasted paper behind the radiator, down both sides of the brackets. Use a radiator roller to press it to the wall (▷). Crease and trim to the skirting board.

Papering around switches and sockets

Turn off the electricity at the mains (▷). Hang the wallcovering over the switch or socket. Make diagonal cuts from the centre of the fitting to each corner. Trim off the waste leaving 6mm (¼in) all round. Loosen the faceplate, tuck the margin behind and retighten it. Don't switch the power back on until the paste is dry. Don't use for foils: the metallic surface can conduct electricity.

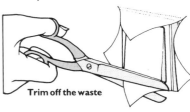

Trim off the waste

SEE ALSO

Details for: ▷	
Consumer unit	78
Radiator roller	75
Preparing plaster	22–23
Wallcoverings	50–51

● **Papering archways**
Arrange strips to leave even gaps between arch sides and the next full-length strips. Hang strips over face of arch, cut curve leaving 25mm (1in) margin. Fold it onto underside snipping into margin to prevent creasing. Fit a strip on the underside to reach from floor to top of arch. Repeat on opposite side of arch.

● **Trimming foils around electrical fittings**
Make diagonal cuts (See left), but crease the waste against the fitting and trim off with a sharp knife when the paste has dried.

55

STAIRWELLS

The only real problem with papering a stairwell is the extra long drops on the side walls. You will need to build a safe work platform over the stairs (◁). Plumb and hang the longest drop first, lapping the head wall above the stairs by 12mm (½in).

Carrying the long drops of wallcovering – sometimes as much as 4.5m (15ft) long – is awkward: paste the covering liberally so it's not likely to dry out while you hang it, then fold it concertina-fashion. Drape it over your arm while you climb the platform. You'll need a helper to support the weight of the pasted length while you apply it. Unfold the flaps as you work down.

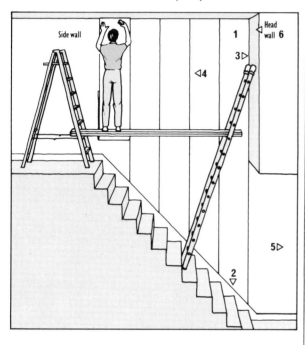

Side wall

Head wall **6**

1

3 ▷

◁**4**

5 ▷

2 ▷

Papering sequence
Follow this sequence for papering a stairwell.
1 Hang the longest drop
2 Crease it into the angled skirting and cut
3 Lap the paper onto the head wall
4, 5 Work away from the first drop in both directions
6 Paper the head wall

Crease and cut the bottom of the paper against the angled skirting. Don't forget – when first you cut the length – to allow for this angle; work to the longest edge measurement. Work away from this first length in both directions, then hang the head wall.

Where the banister rail is let into the stairwell wall, try to arrange the rolls so that the rail falls between the two butted drops. Hang the drops to the rail and cut horizontally into the edge of the last strip at the centre of the rail, then make radial cuts so the paper can be moulded around the rail. Crease the flaps, peel away the wallcovering and cut them off. Smooth the covering back.

Hang the next drop at the other side of the rail, butting it to the previous piece and make similar radial cuts.

SPECIAL TECHNIQUES FOR WALLPAPERING

Whatever you are using as a wallcovering, follow the standard wallpapering techniques as explained previously. However, there are some additional considerations and special techniques involved in using certain types of wallcovering, as explained below and opposite.

RELIEF WALLCOVERINGS

When hanging *Anaglypta*, line the wall first and use a heavy-duty paste. Apply the paste liberally and evenly but try not to leave too much paste in the depressions. Allow it to soak for 10 minutes. *Supaglypta* will need 15 minutes soaking time.

Don't use a seam roller on the joins: tap the paper gently with a paperhanger's brush to avoid flattening the embossing.

Don't turn a relief wallcovering around corners. Measure the distance from the last drop to the corner and cut your next length to fit. Trim and hang the offcut to meet at the corner. Fill external corners with cellulose filler once the paper has dried thoroughly.

To use *Lincrusta*, sponge the back with hot water until it is thoroughly soaked. Apply the paste and hang the length, rubbing it down with a felt or rubber roller.

Use a sharp knife and straightedge to trim *Lincrusta*. Treat the corners with filler as for *Anaglypta*.

VINYL WALLCOVERINGS

Paste paper-backed vinyls in the normal way, but cotton-backed vinyl hangs better if you paste the wall and leave it to become tacky before applying the wallcovering. Use fungicidal paste.

Hang and butt join lengths of vinyl using a sponge to smooth them onto the wall rather than a brush. Crease a length top and bottom, then trim it to size with a sharp knife.

Vinyl will not stick to itself, so when you turn a corner, use a knife to cut through both pieces of paper where they overlap. Peel away the excess and rub down the vinyl to produce a perfect butt join.

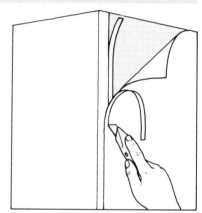

Cut through overlap and remove excess

READY-PASTED WALLCOVERINGS

Place the trough of cold water next to the skirting at the position of the first drop. Roll a cut length loosely from the bottom with the pattern on the outside. Immerse the roll in the trough for the prescribed time, according to the manufacturer's instructions.

Take hold of the cut end and lift the paper, allowing it to unroll naturally, draining the surface water back into the trough at the same time.

Hang and butt join the coverings in the usual way — use a sponge to apply vinyls but use a paperhanger's brush for other coverings.

Hanging a long wet length can be difficult if you follow the standard procedure. Instead, roll the length from the top with the pattern outermost. Place it in the trough and immediately re-roll it through the water. Take it from the trough in roll form and drain excess water. Hang it by feeding from the roll as you proceed.

Pull paper from trough and hang on the wall

SPECIAL TECHNIQUES FOR WALLPAPERING

UNBACKED FABRICS

METALLIC FOILS

The acid content of old paste may discolour metallic foil papers, so coat either the paper or the wall with fresh fungicidal paste.

FLOCK PAPER

Protect the flocking with a piece of lining paper and remove air bubbles with a paperhanger's brush. Cut through both

FOAMED POLYETHYLENE

Novamura (foamed polyethylene) can be hung straight from the roll onto a pasted wall. Sponge in place and trim it top and bottom with scissors.

thicknesses of overlapped joins and remove the surplus; press back the edges to make a neat butt join.

FABRICS AND SPECIAL COVERINGS

Try to keep paste off the face of paper-backed fabrics and any other special wallcoverings. There are so many different coverings, so check with the supplier which paste to use.

So you don't damage a delicate surface, use a felt or rubber roller to press in place or stipple with a brush.

Most fabric coverings will be machine-trimmed but if the edges are

frayed, overlap the joints and cut through both thicknesses then peel off the waste to make a butt join. Make a similar join at a corner.

Many fabrics are sold in wide rolls: even one cut length will be heavy and awkward to handle. Paste the wall, then support the rolled length on a batten between two stepladders. Work from the bottom upwards.

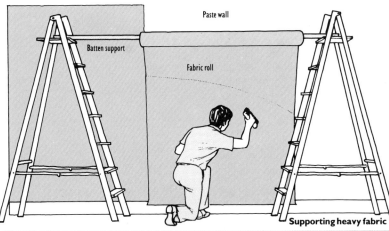

Paste wall

Batten support

Fabric roll

Supporting heavy fabric

GLASS FIBRE WALLCOVERINGS

Hang glass fibre coverings by applying the special adhesive to the wall with a roller. Hang and butt the lengths, then use a spatula to smooth the covering from the centre outwards (or use a felt or rubber roller).

Crease and trim glass fibre as for ordinary wallcoverings, or use a knife and straightedge. Leave the glue to set for 24 hours, then paint. When the first coat has dried, lightly rub down to remove raised fibres, then recoat.

EXPANDED POLYSTYRENE

Paint or roll special adhesive onto the wall. Hang the covering straight from the roll, smooth gently with the flat of your hand, then roll over it lightly with a dry paint roller.

If the edge is square, butt adjacent drops. If it is crushed or crumbled, overlap the join and cut through both

thicknesses with a sharp trimming knife, peel away the offcuts and rub the edges down. Unless the edges are generously glued, they will curl apart. Trim top and bottom with a knife and straightedge. Allow the adhesive to dry for 72 hours then hang the wallcovering using a thick fungicidal paste.

If you want to apply a plain coloured medium-weight fabric, you can glue it directly to the wall. However, it is easy to stretch an unbacked fabric so that aligning a pattern is difficult.

For more control, stretch the fabric onto 12mm (½in) thick panels of lightweight insulation board (you'll then have the added advantage of insulation and a pin-board). Stick the boards directly onto the wall.

Using paste
Test an offcut of the fabric first to make sure that the adhesive will not stain it. Use a ready-mixed paste and roll it onto the wall.

Wrap a cut length of fabric around a cardboard tube (from a carpet supplier) and gradually unroll it on the surface, smoothing it down with a dry paint roller. Take care not to distort the weave. Overlap the joins but do not cut through them until the paste has dried, in case the fabric shrinks. Re-paste and close the seam.

Press the fabric into the ceiling line and skirting and trim away the excess with a sharp trimming knife when the paste has set.

Making wall panels
Cut the insulation board to suit the width of the fabric and the height of the wall. Stretch the fabric across the panel, wrap it around the edges, then use latex adhesive to stick it to the back. Hold it temporarily with drawing pins, while the adhesive dries.

Either use wallboard adhesive to glue the panels to the wall or pin them, tapping the nail heads through the weave of the fabric to conceal them.

SEE ALSO

Details for: ▷	
Preparing plaster	22–23
Wallcoverings	50–51
Felt/rubber roller	77

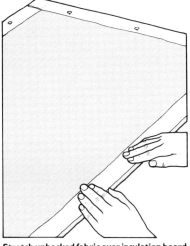

Stretch unbacked fabric over insulation board

PAPERING A CEILING

Papering a ceiling isn't as difficult as you may think: the techniques are basically the same as for papering a wall, except that the drops are usually longer and more unwieldy to hold while you brush the paper into place. Set up a sensible work platform — it's virtually impossible to work by moving a single stepladder along – and enlist a helper to support the pasted, folded paper while you position one end, and progress backwards across the room. If you've marked out the ceiling first, the result should be faultless.

Setting out the ceiling

Arrange your work platform (◁) before you begin to plan out the papering sequence for the ceiling. The best type of platform to use is a purpose-made decorator's trestle, but you can manage with a scaffold board spanning between two pairs of stepladders.

Now mark the ceiling to give a visual guide to positioning the strips of paper. Aim to work parallel with the window wall and away from the light, so you can see what you are doing and so that the light will not highlight the joins between strips. If the distance is shorter the other way, hang the strips in that direction for ease.

Mark a guide line along the ceiling, one roll-width minus 12mm (½in) from the side wall, so that the first strip of paper will lap onto the wall.

Working from a ladder
If you have to work from a stepladder, an assistant can support the paper on a cardboard tube taped to a broom.

Putting up the paper

Paste and fold the paper as for wallcovering, concertina fashion (◁), drape it over a spare roll and carry it to the work platform. You'll certainly find it easier to get a helper to hold the folded paper, giving you both hands free for brushing into place.

Hold the strip against the guideline, using a brush to stroke it onto the ceiling. Tap it into the wall angle then gradually work backwards along the scaffold board, brushing on the paper as your helper unfolds it.

If the ceiling has a cornice, crease and trim the paper at the ends. Otherwise, leave it to lap the walls by 12mm (½in) so that it will be covered by the wallcovering. Work across the ceiling in the same way, butting the lengths of paper together. Cut the final strip to roughly the width, and trim into the wall angle.

Papering a ceiling
The job is so much easier if two people work together.
1 Mark guide line on ceiling
2 Support folded paper on tube
3 Brush on paper, from centre outwards
4 Overlap covered by wallpaper
5 Use two boards to support two people

There are usually few obstructions on a ceiling to make papering difficult – unlike walls, which have doors, windows and radiators to contend with. The only problem areas occur where there's a pendant light fitting or a decorative plaster centrepiece.

Cutting around a pendant light
Where the paper passes over a ceiling rose, cut several triangular flaps so that you can pass the light fitting through the hole. Tap the paper all round the rose with a paperhanging brush and continue to the end of the strip. Return to the rose and cut off the flaps with a knife.

Papering around a centrepiece
If you have a decorative plaster centrepiece, work out the position of the strips so that a joint will pass through the middle. Cut long flaps from the side of each piece of paper so that you can tuck it in all round the plaster moulding.

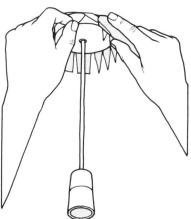

Cut off triangular flaps when paste is dry

Cut long strips to fit around moulding

CHOOSING TILES

Tiling is a universally popular method of decorating a surface, with an almost inexhaustible range of colours, textures and patterns to choose from depending on the degree of durability required. Tiling provides the facility of finishing a surface with small, regular units which can be cut and fitted into an awkward shape far easier than sheet materials.

Glazed ceramic tiles

Hard ceramic tiles, usually glazed and fired, are made for walls and floors. Unglazed tiles are available but only to provide a surer grip for flooring. A textured surface reduces the risk of accidents where a floor might become wet. All ceramic tiles are durable and waterproof, but be sure to use special heat- and frost-resistant tiles where appropriate. Do not use wall tiles on the floor as they cannot take the weight of traffic or furniture.

The majority of tiles are square but dimensions vary according to use and the manufacturer's preference. Rectangular and more irregular shaped tiles are available. Typical shapes include hexagons, octagons, diamonds and interlocking units with curved elaborate edges. Other units include slim rectangles with pointed (pic) or slanted (cane) ends. Use them in combination to produce patterned floors and walls.

Mosaic tiles

Mosaic tiles are small versions of the standard ceramic tiles. To lay them individually would be time consuming and lead to inaccuracy, so they are usually joined by a paper covering, or a mesh background, into larger panels. Square tiles are common but rectangular, hexagonal and round mosaics are also available. Because they are small, mosaics can be used on curved surfaces, and will fit irregular shapes better than large ceramic tiles.

Quarry tiles

Quarry tiles are thick, unglazed ceramic tiles used for floors which need a hardwearing, waterproof surface. Colours are limited to browns, reds, black and white. Machine-made tiles are regular in size and even in colour but hand-made tiles are variable, producing a beautiful mottled effect. Quarry tiles are difficult to cut so do not use them where you will have to fit them against a complicated shape. Rounded-edge quarry tiles can be used as treads for steps, and a floor can be finished with skirting tiles.

Stone and slate flooring

A floor laid with real stone or slate tiles will be exquisite but expensive. Sizes and thicknesses will vary according to the manufacturer – some will even cut to measure. A few materials are so costly that you should consider hiring a professional to lay them, otherwise treat cheaper ones like quarry tiles.

SEE ALSO

Details for: ▷	
Choosing colour/pattern	6–7, 11
Preparing plaster	22–23
Wall tiling	62–64
Floor tiling	70–71

Standard tile sections
A range of sections is produced for specific functions:

Field tile for general tiling with spacing lugs moulded onto them.

Rounded-edge (RE) tile for edging the field.

REX tile with two adjacent rounded edges.

Universal tile with two glazed, square edges for use in any position.

Tile selection
The examples shown left are a typical cross-section of commercially available ceramic tiles.
1 Glazed ceramic
2 Shape and size variation
3 Mosaic tiles
4 Quarry tiles
5 Slate and stone

CHOOSING TILES

Stone and brick tiles

Thin masonry facing tiles can be used to simulate a stone or brick wall as a feature area for a chimney breast, for example, or to clad a whole wall. Stone tiles are typically made from reconstituted stone in moulds, and most look unconvincing as an imitation of the real thing. Colour choice is intended to reflect local stone types, and is typically white, grey or buff. Some 'weathered' versions are also made.

Brick tiles look much more authentic. The best ones are actually brick 'slips' – slivers cut from kiln-produced bricks. A very wide range of traditional brick colours is available.

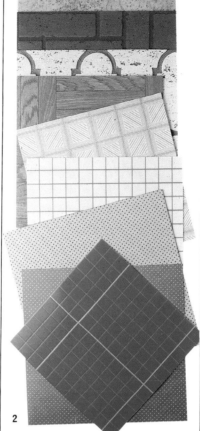

2

Vinyl tiles

Vinyl tiles are among the cheapest and easiest floorcoverings to use. Vinyl can be cut easily, and so long as the tiles are firmly glued, with good joints, the floor will be waterproof. However, it will still be susceptible to scorching. A standard coated tile has a printed pattern between a vinyl backing and a harder, clear vinyl surface. Solid vinyl tiles are made entirely of the hardwearing plastic. Some vinyl tiles have a high proportion of mineral filler. As a result they are stiff and must be laid on a perfectly flat base. Unlike standard vinyl tiles, they will resist some rising damp in a concrete sub-floor. Most tiles are square or rectangular but there are interlocking shapes and hexagons. There are many patterns and colours to choose from, including embossed vinyl which represents ceramic, brick or stone tiling.

CARPET TILES

Carpet tiles have advantages over wall-to-wall carpeting. There is less to fear when cutting a single tile to fit, and, being loose-laid, a worn, burnt or stained tile can be replaced instantly. However, you can't substitute a brand new tile several years later, as the colour will not match. Buy several spares initially and swap them around regularly to even out the wear and colour change. Most types of carpet are available as tiles, including cord, loop and twist piles in wool as well as a range of man-made fibres. Tiles are normally plain in colour but some are patterned to give a striking grid effect. Some tiles have an integral rubber underlay.

A selection of carpet tiles
Tiles are used extensively for contract carpeting but they are equally suitable as a hard-wearing floor covering in the home.

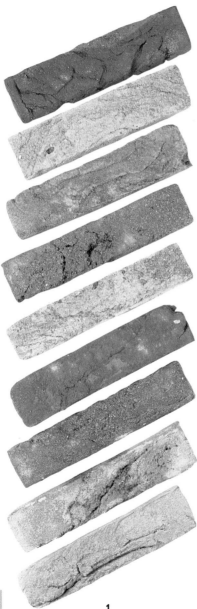

Left to right
1 Brick tiles
2 Vinyl floor tiles

1

CHOOSING TILES

Polystyrene tiles

Although expanded polystyrene tiles will not reduce heat loss from a room by any significant amount, they will deter condensation as well as mask a ceiling in poor condition. Polystyrene cuts easily so long as the trimming knife is very sharp. For safety in case of fire, choose a self-extinguishing type and do not overpaint with an oil paint. Wall tiles are made but they will crush easily and aren't suitable for use in a vulnerable area. There are flat or decoratively-embossed tiles.

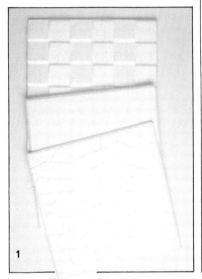

Mirror tiles

Square and rectangular mirror tiles can be attached to walls with self-adhesive pads in each corner. There is a choice of silver, bronze or smoke grey finish. Don't expect tiles to produce a perfect reflection unless they are mounted on a really flat surface.

Mineral fibre tiles

Ceiling tiles made from compressed mineral fibre are dense enough to be sound and heat insulating. They often have tongued-and-grooved edges so that, once stapled to the ceiling, the next interlocking tile covers the fixings. Fibre tiles can also be glued directly to a flat ceiling. A range of textured surfaces is available.

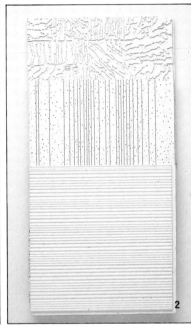

Metal tiles

Lightweight pressed metal tiles are fixed in the same way as mirror tiles. Choose from aluminium, bronze and gold coloured tiles with satin or bright finishes. These tiles are not grouted so do not use them where food particles can gather in the crevices.

Rubber tiles

Soft rubber tiles were originally made for use in shops and offices, but they are equally suitable for the home, being hardwearing yet soft and quiet to walk on. The surface is usually studded or textured to improve the grip. Choice is limited to a few plain colours.

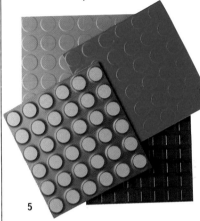

Cork tiles

Cork is a popular covering for walls and floors. It is easy to lay with contact adhesive and can be cut to size and shape with a knife. There's a wide range of textures and warm colours to choose from. Pre-sanded but unfinished cork will darken in tone when you varnish it. Alternatively, you can buy ready-finished tiles with various plastic and wax coatings. Soft, granular insulating cork is suitable as a decorative finish for walls only. It crumbles easily, so should not be used where it will be exposed on external corners.

SEE ALSO

Details for: ▷	
Choosing colour/pattern	6–7, 11
Preparing plaster	22–23
Wall tiling	65
Floor tiling	67–69

Left to right
1 Polystyrene tiles
2 Mineral fibre tiles
3 Mirror tiles
4 Metal wall tiles
5 Rubber tiles
6 Cork floor tiles

SETTING OUT FOR WALL TILES

Whatever tiles you plan to use, the walls must be clean, sound and dry. You cannot tile over wallpaper, and flaking or powdery paint must be treated first to give a suitably stable base for the tiles. It's important that you make the surface as flat as possible so the tiles will stick firmly. Setting out the prepared surface accurately is a vital aid to hanging the tiles properly.

MAKING A GAUGE STICK

First make a gauge stick (a tool for plotting the position of tiles on the wall) from a length of 50 x 12mm (2 x ½in) softwood. Lay several tiles along it, butting together those with lugs, or add spacers for square-edged tiles, unless they're intended to be close-butted. Mark the position of each tile on the softwood batten.

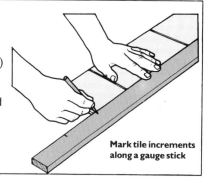

Mark tile increments along a gauge stick

Setting out a plain wall

On a plain uninterrupted wall, use the gauge stick to plan horizontal rows starting at skirting level. If you are left with a narrow strip at the top, move the rows up half a tile-width to create a wider margin. Mark the bottom of the lowest row of whole tiles. Temporarily nail a thin guide batten to the wall aligned with the mark (**1**). Make sure it is horizontal by placing a level on top.

Mark the centre of the wall (**2**), then use the gauge stick to set out the vertical rows at each side of it. If the border tiles are less than half a width, reposition the rows sideways by half a tile. Use a spirit level to position a guide batten against the last vertical line and nail it (**3**).

Plotting a half-tiled wall

If you are tiling part of a wall only, up to a dado rail for instance, set out the tiles with a row of whole tiles at the top (**4**).

This is even more important if you are using RE or REX tiles which are used for the top row of a half-tiled wall.

Arranging tiles around a window

Use a window as your starting point so that the tiles surrounding it are equal and not too narrow. If possible, begin a row of whole tiles at sill level (**5**), and position cut tiles at the back of a window reveal (**6**). Fix a guide batten over a window to support the rows of tiles temporarily (**7**).

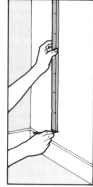

Using a gauge stick
Hold a home-made gauge stick firmly against the wall and mark the positions of the tiles on the surface.

Setting out for tiling
Plan out the tiling arrangement on the walls as shown right, but first plot the symmetry of the tile field with a gauge stick to ensure a wide margin all round.
1 Temporarily fix a horizontal batten at the base of the field
2 Mark the centre of the wall
3 Gauge from the mark then fix a vertical batten to indicate the side of the field
4 Start under a dado rail with whole tiles
5 Use a row of whole tiles at sill level
6 Place cut tiles at back of a reveal
7 Support tiles over window while they set

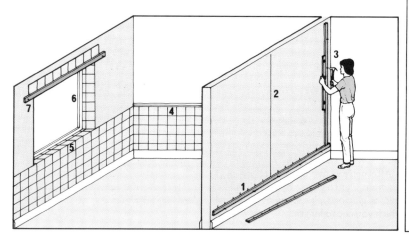

RENOVATING TILES

A properly tiled surface should last for many years but the appearance is often spoiled by one or two damaged tiles, by discoloured grouting on ceramic tiles, lifting or curling of cork, vinyl or polystyrene tiles. There is usually no need to redecorate – most problems can be solved fairly easily.

Renewing the grouting
It's not necessary to rake out old, drab grouting: use a renovation kit to brighten up the existing grout.

Brush on the liquid colourant (supplied in red, white, blue, green, beige or brown), following the lines of the grout which must be clean and dry. After about an hour, wet the area with a sponge, leave it for three minutes, then wipe excess colourant from the tiles. The liquid forms a strong bond with the grout and provides a water-resistant finish which can be polished with a dry cloth if required.

Replacing a cracked ceramic tile
Scrape the grout from around the damaged tiles then use a fine cold chisel to carefully chip out the tile, working from the centre. Take care not to dislodge its neighbours.

Scrape out the remains of the adhesive and vacuum the recess. Butter the back of the replacement tile with adhesive then press it firmly in place. Wipe off excess adhesive, allow it to set, then renew the grouting.

Lifting a cork or vinyl floor tile
Try to remove a single tile by chopping it out from the centre with a wood chisel. If the adhesive is firm, try warming the tile with a domestic iron.

Scrape the floor clean of old adhesive and try the new tile for fit. Trim the edges if necessary. Spread adhesive on the floor, then place one corner of the tile in position. Gradually lower it into the recess. Spread the tile with your finger tips to squeeze out any air bubbles, place a heavy weight on it and leave overnight.

Removing a ceiling tile
Loosen a polystyrene tile by picking it out from the centre with a sharp knife and paint scraper. Don't lever it out or you will crush the adjoining tile. Stick the replacement tile back on a complete bed of special adhesive. Remove a stapled ceiling tile by cutting through the tongues all round.

TILING A WALL: CERAMIC TILES

Choosing the correct adhesive

Most ceramic tile adhesives are sold ready-mixed, although a few need to be mixed with water. Tubs or packets will state the coverage.

A standard adhesive is suitable for most applications but use a waterproof type in areas likely to be subjected to running water or splashing. If the tiles are to be laid on a wallboard, use a flexible adhesive and make sure it is heat resistant for worktops or around a fireplace. Some adhesives can also be used for grouting the finished wall.

A notched plastic spreader is usually supplied with each tub, or you can use a serrated trowel.

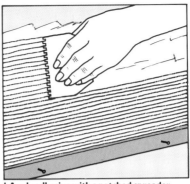

I Apply adhesive with a notched spreader

Hanging the tiles

Spread enough adhesive on the wall to cover about one metre square (about 3ft square). Press the teeth of the spreader against the surface and drag it through the adhesive so that it forms horizontal ridges (**1**).

Press the first tile into the angle formed by the setting-out battens (**2**) until it is firmly fixed, then butt up tiles on each side. Build up three or four rows at a time. If the tiles do not have lugs, place matchsticks, thick card or proprietary plastic spacers between them to form the grout lines. Wipe away adhesive from the surface with a damp sponge.

Spread more adhesive and tile along the batten until the first rows of whole tiles are complete. From time to time, check that your tiling is accurate by holding a batten and spirit level across the faces and along the top and edge. When you have completed the entire field, scrape adhesive from the border and allow it to set before removing the setting-out battens.

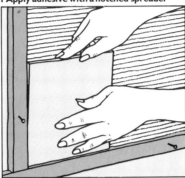

2 Stick first tile in angle of 'setting-out' battens

Ceramic coving tiles

Quadrant
Used to fill the joint between bath and wall

Mitred tile
Use at the end if you want to turn a corner

Bullnose tile
Use this tile to finish the end of a straight run

Grouting tiles and sealing joins

Use a ready-mixed paste called grout to fill the gaps between the tiles. Standard grout is white, grey or brown, but there is also a range of coloured grouts to match or contrast with the tiles. Alternatively, mix pigments with dry, powdered grout before adding water to match any colour.

Waterproof grout is essential for showers and bath surrounds, and you should use an epoxy-based grout for worktops to keep them germ-free.

Leave the adhesive to harden for 24 hours, then use a rubber-bladed squeegee or plastic scraper to press the grout into the joins (**3**). Spread it in all directions to make sure all joins are well filled.

Wipe grout from the surface of the tiles with a sponge before it sets and smooth the joins with a blunt-ended stick – a dowel will do.

When the grout has dried, polish the tiles with a dry cloth. Do not use a tiled shower for about seven days to let the grout harden thoroughly.

3 Press grout into joins with rubber squeegee

Sealing around bathroom fittings

Don't use grout or ordinary filler to seal the gap between a tiled wall and shower tray, bath or basin: the fittings can flex enough to crack a rigid seal, and frequent soakings will allow water to seep in, create stains and damage the floor and wall. Use a silicone rubber caulking compound to fill the gaps; it remains flexible enough to accommodate any movement.

Sealants are sold in a choice of colours to match popular tile and sanitaryware colourways. They come in tubes or cartridges and can cope with gaps up to 3mm (⅛in) wide: over that, pack out with soft rope or twists of soaked newspaper.

If you're using a tube, trim the end off the plastic nozzle and press the tip into the joint at an angle of 45 degrees. Push forward at a steady rate while squeezing the tube to apply a bead of sealant. Smooth any ripples with the back of a wetted teaspoon.

If you're using a cartridge, again, snip the end off the angled nozzle – the amount you cut off dictates the thickness of the bead – and use the container's finger-action dispenser to squirt out the sealant (**4**).

Alternatively, use ceramic coving or quadrant tiles to edge a bath or shower unit, or glue on a plastic coving strip which you cut to length.

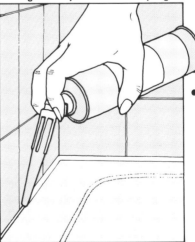

4 Seal between tiles and fittings with sealant

● **Tiling around pipes and fittings**
Check with the gauge stick how the tiles will fit round socket outlets and switches, pipes and other obstructions. Make slight adjustments to the position of the main field to avoid difficult shaping around these features.

CUTTING CERAMIC TILES

Having finished the main field of tiles you will have to cut the ceramic tiles to fill the border and to fit around obstructions such as window frames, *electrical fittings, pipes and the basin. Making straight cuts is easy using a purpose-made cutter but shaping tiles to fit curves takes practice.*

Cutting thin strips
A cutting jig is the most accurate way to cut a thin strip cleanly from the edge of a tile. If you do not want to use the strip itself, nibble away the waste a little at a time with pincers or special tile nibblers.

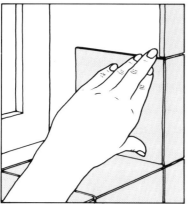

Tiling around a window
Tile up to the edges of a window, then stick RE tiles to the reveal so that they lap the edges of surrounding tiles. Fill in behind the edging tiles with cut tiles.

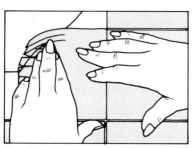

Cutting a curve
To fit a tile against a curved shape, cut a template from thin card to the exact size of a tile. Cut 'fingers' along one edge; press them against the curve to reproduce the shape. Transfer the curve onto the face of the tile and score the line freehand. Nibble away the waste a little at a time using pincers or a tile nibbler and smooth the edge with a slipstone.

Tile cutting jig
A worthwhile investment if you're cutting a lot of tiles, a proprietary jig incorporates a device for measuring and scoring tiles. The cutter is drawn down the channel of the adjustable guide. The tile is snapped with a special pincer-action tool.

Mark two edges   **Cut and fit tile**

Fitting around a pipe
Mark the centre of the pipe on the top and side edges of a tile and draw lines across the tile from these points. Where they cross, draw round a coin or something slightly larger than the diameter of the pipe.

Make one straight cut through the centre of the circle and either nibble out the waste, having scored the curve, or clamp it in a vice, protected with softening, and cut it out with a saw file – a thin rod coated with hard, abrasive particles which will cut in any direction. Stick one half of the tile on each side of the pipe.

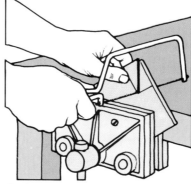

Fitting around a socket or switch
In order to fit around a socket or switch you may have to cut the corner out of a tile. Mark it from the socket then clamp the tile in a vice, protected with softening. Score both lines then use a saw file to make one diagonal cut from the corner of the tile to where the lines meet. Snap out both triangles.

If you have to cut a notch out of a large tile, cut down both sides with a hacksaw then score between them and snap the piece out of the middle.

CUTTING BORDER TILES

It's necessary to cut border tiles one at a time to fit the gap between the field tiles and the adjacent wall: walls are rarely truly square and the margin is bound to be uneven.

Making straight cuts
Mark a border tile by placing it face down over its neighbour with one edge against the adjacent wall (**1**). Make an allowance for normal spacing between the tiles. Transfer the marks to the edge of the tiles using a felt-tip pen.

Use a proprietary tile cutter held against a straightedge to score across the face with one firm stroke to cut through the glaze (**2**). You may have to score the edge of thick tiles.

Stretch a length of thin wire across a panel of chipboard, place the scored line directly over the wire and press down on both sides to snap the tile (**3**).

Alternatively use a tile cutter, which has a wheel to score the tile and jaws to snap it along the line. If you're doing a lot of tiling, invest in a purpose-made jig. The jig will hold the tile square with a cutting edge; pressing down on the guide snaps the tile cleanly. Some jigs include a device for measuring border tiles, too.

Smooth the cut edges of the tile with a tile sander or small slipstone (◁).

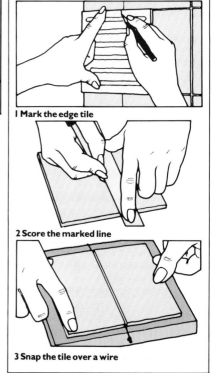

1 Mark the edge tile

2 Score the marked line

3 Snap the tile over a wire

Mosaic tiles

Ceramic mosaic tiles are applied to a wall in a similar way to large square tiles. Set out the wall (▷) and use the same adhesive and grout.

The mesh backing on some sheets is pressed into the adhesive. The facing paper on other sheets is left intact on the surface until the adhesive sets.

Fill the main area of the wall, spacing the sheets to equal the gaps between individual tiles. Place a carpet-covered board over the sheets and tap it with a mallet to bed the tiles into the adhesive.

Fill borders by cutting strips from the sheet. Cut individual tiles to fit into awkward shapes and around fittings. If necessary, soak off the facing paper with a damp sponge and grout the tiles (▷).

Bedding mosaics
Bed tiles by tapping a carpet-covered board.

Mirror tiles

Set out the wall with battens (▷) but avoid using mirror tiles in an area which would entail complicated fitting, as it is difficult to cut glass except in straight lines. Mirror tiles are fixed, close-butted, with self-adhesive pads. No grout is necessary.

Peel the protective paper from the pads and lightly position each tile. Check its alignment with a spirit level then press it firmly into place with a soft cloth.

Use a wooden straightedge and a wheel glass cutter to score a line across a tile. Make one firm stroke. Lay the tile over a stretched wire and press down on both sides. Remove the sharp cut edge with an oiled slipstone.

Add spare pads and fix the tile in place. Finally, polish the tiles to remove any unsightly fingermarks.

Placing mirror tiles
Position tile before pressing on wall.

Metal tiles

Set out metallic tiles as for ceramic ones. No adhesive or grout is required. Don't fit metal tiles behind electrical fittings – there's a risk that they could conduct the current.

Remove the protective paper from the adhesive pads on the back and press each tile onto the wall. Check the alignment of the tiles regularly: they are not always perfectly made.

Cut border tiles with scissors or tinsnips, but nick the edges before cutting across the face or the surface is likely to distort.

To round over a cut edge, cut a wooden block to fit inside the tile, and align it with the edge. Tap and rub along the edge with another block.

To fit into a corner, file a V-shape into the opposite edges then bend the tile over the edge of the table.

When the wall is complete, peel off any protective film, which may be covering the tiles.

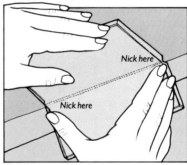

Bending metal tiles
Nick the edges of metal tiles before bending.

Cork tiles

Set up a horizontal guide batten (▷) to make sure you lay the tiles accurately. It isn't necessary to fix a vertical batten, however; the large tiles are easy to align without one. Simply mark a vertical line centrally on the wall and hang the tiles in both directions from it.

Use a rubber-based contact adhesive to fix cork tiles, if possible the type that allows a degree of movement when positioning them. If any adhesive gets onto the surface of a tile, clean it off immediately with a suitable solvent such as acetone on a cloth.

Spread adhesive thinly and evenly onto the wall and back of the tiles and leave it to dry. Lay each tile by placing one edge only against the batten or its neighbour then gradually press the rest of the tile onto the wall. Smooth it down with your palms.

Cut cork tiles with a sharp trimming knife. Because the edges are butted tightly, you'll need to be very accurate when marking out border tiles. Use the same method as for laying cork and vinyl floor tiles (▷). Cut and fit curved shapes using a template.

Unless the tiles are pre-coated, apply two coats of varnish after 24 hours.

Tiling around curves

In many older houses some walls might be rounded at the external corners. Flexible tiles such as vinyl, rubber and carpet types are easy to bend into quite tight radiuses, but cork will snap if bent too far.

Cut a series of shallow slits vertically down the back of a tile within its central section, using a tenon saw, then bend it gently to the curve required.

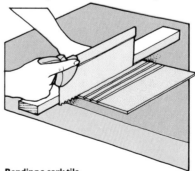

Bending a cork tile
Cut a series of shallow slits vertically down the back of a tile using a tenon saw within the central section, then bend it gently: the slits will enable the tile to assume even a fairly tight curve without snapping, but experiment first.

FIXING BRICK TILES

Brick tiles can look quite authentic if laid in a standard running bond (◁), although you need not be hampered by structural requirements: you can hang them vertically, horizontally, diagonally or even in zig-zag fashion to achieve a dramatic effect.

You can either leave the skirting in place and start the first course of tiles just above it, or remove the skirting and replace it just lapping over the bottom course of tiles. Alternatively, remove the skirting and set a row of brick tiles on end.

Applying adhesive
Butter the tile back using a notched spreader.

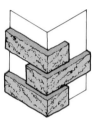

Corner tiles
Start with three corner tiles at each end of a run.

Fixing brick tiles
Follow this procedure when fixing brick tiles to your wall.
1 Plot the tile courses vertically and horizontally with two gauge sticks. Allow joint spaces between each tile
2 Use pre-formed tiles at external corners
3 Set a course of tiles on end above a window as a brick lintel
4 Set the bottom row of tiles on the skirting on the new wall suface or substitute with a row of brick tiles on end
5 Leave a gap for ventilating the flue in a blocked off fireplace
6 Fix tiles from the bottom up, staggering the vertical joints

Setting out the wall

Make two gauge sticks, one for the vertical coursing and another to space the tiles sideways. Allow 10mm (⅜in) spacing between each tile for the mortar joints, but adjust this slightly so there will be a full-width tile top and bottom.

Work out your spacing side to side so that, if possible, you have one course of whole tiles, alternating with courses containing a half tile at each end.

If you are using corner tiles at each end, work out your spacing from them towards the middle of a wall, and place cut tiles centrally.

Gluing on the tiles

You can use mortar to stick brick tiles to the wall but most types are sold with a compatible adhesive. Use a notched spreader to coat the back of each tile (left), then press it on the wall. Some manufacturers recommend spreading the adhesive onto the wall, instead of the tile.

If you are using pre-formed corner tiles, fix them first, three at a time, alternating headers and stretchers (◁). Check that they are level at each side of the wall with a batten and spirit level

Fitting around a window
Lay tiles vertically above a window in a 'soldier course' to simulate a brick lintel. Use prefabricated corner tiles to take the brickwork into a window reveal for the most realistic effect.

Cutting brick tiles
Most brick tiles can be cut with a hacksaw, but if a cut edge looks too sharp, round it over by rubbing with a scrap piece of tile. You can also cut tiles using a club hammer and bolster chisel, and the thinnest type can even be cut with scissors.

then fill in between.

Start filling in by tiling the bottom course, using small 10mm (⅜in) wooden offcuts to space the tiles: some tiles come with polystyrene packing, which you should cut into pieces to use as spacers. Every third course, use a spirit level to check the alignment of the tiles, and adjust if necessary.

STONE TILES

Stone tiles are laid in the same way as brick tiles. Coursed stones should be arranged with a selection of small and large tiles for the most authentic look: lay the tiles on the floor to plan the setting out, then transfer them to the wall one by one.

Irregularly-shaped stones can be laid in any pattern you want, but again, it's best to set them out on the floor to achieve a good balance of large and small sizes for realism.

With some stone tiles you have to coat the wall with a special mortar-coloured adhesive, which gives an overall background, then stick the individual tiles on by buttering their backs with adhesive.

Bending brick tiles
Most brick tiles are made from rigid ceramic but some plastic tiles can be hand bent around a corner or even a curved column. Heat the tile gently with a hot air stripper or hair dryer until it is pliable. Wearing thick gloves, grasp the tile and bend it round the angle.

Pointing the joints
After 24 hours, use a ready-mixed mortar to point the wall as if it was real brickwork. Brush smears of mortar from the faces of the tiles with a stiff-bristled brush.

If you don't want to point the joints, simply leave them as they are: the adhesive is coloured to resemble mortar and the wall will look as though it has been finished with raked joints.

SETTING OUT FOR DIAGONAL TILING

Arranging the tiles diagonally can create an unusual decorative effect, especially if your choice of tiles enables you to mix colours. Setting out and laying the tiles off centre isn't complicated – it's virtually the same as fixing them at right-angles, except that you'll be working into a corner instead of a wall. Mark a centre line, and bisect it at right-angles using an improvised compass (right). Draw a line from opposite diagonal corners of the room through the centre point. Dry lay a row of tiles to plot the margins (See below). Mark a right-angle to the diagonal. Fix a batten along one diagonal as a guide to laying the first row of tiles.

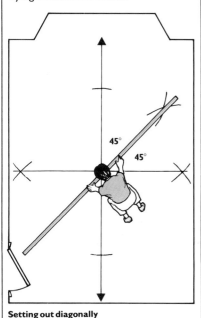

Setting out diagonally
Bisect the quartered room at 45 degrees

SETTING OUT FOR SOFT FLOOR TILES

Vinyl, rubber, cork and carpet tiles are relatively large, so you can complete the floor fairly quickly. Some vinyl tiles are self-adhesive, and carpet tiles are loose-laid, both of which speed up the process still further. Soft tiles such as these can be cut easily with a sharp trimming knife or even scissors, so fitting to irregular shapes is easier.

Marking out the floor

You can lay tiles onto a solid concrete or suspended wooden floor, so long as the surface is level, clean and dry. Most soft tiles can be set out in a similar way: find the centre of two opposite walls, snap a chalked string between them to mark a line across the floor **(1)**. Lay loose tiles at right-angles to the line up to one wall (see below left). If there is a gap of less than half a tile-width, move the line sideways by half a tile to give a wider margin.

To draw a line at right-angles to the first, use string and a pencil as an improvised compass to scribe arcs on the marked line, at equal distances each side of the centre **(2)**.

From each point, scribe arcs on both sides of the line **(3)**, which bisect each other. Join the points to form a line across the room **(4)**. As before, lay tiles at right-angles to the new line to make sure border tiles are at least half width. Nail a guide batten against one line to align the first row of tiles.

If the room is noticeably irregular in shape, centre the first line on the fireplace or the door opening (see below right).

SEE ALSO

Details for: ▷
Floor tiles   60–61

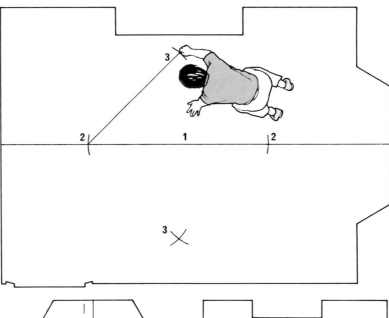

Setting out
When marked out, the quartered room ensures that the tiles can be laid symmetrically. This method is suitable for the following tiles: vinyl, rubber, cork, carpet.

4 Right angle complete

Plotting margin width *(near right)*
Lay loose tiles to make sure there is a reasonable gap at the margins. If not, move the line half a tile-width to the left.

Plotting an odd-shaped room *(far right)*
When a room is not a single rectangle, set out the lines using the fireplace and door as focal points.

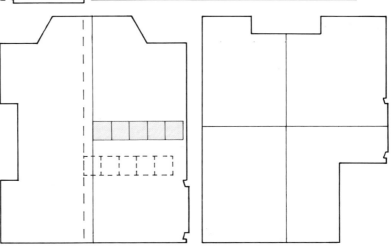

67

LAYING VINYL FLOOR TILES

Tiles pre-coated with adhesive can be laid quickly and simply, plus there is no risk of squeezing glue onto the surface. If you're not using *self-adhesive tiles, however, follow the tile manufacturer's instructions concerning the type of adhesive to use.*

Fixing self-adhesive tiles

Stack the tiles in the room for 24 hours before you lay them so they become properly acclimatized.

If the tiles have a directional pattern – some have arrows printed on the back to indicate this – make sure you lay them the correct way.

Remove the protective paper backing from the first tile prior to laying (1), then press the edge against the guide

batten. Align one corner with the centre line (2). Gradually lower the tile onto the floor and press it down.

Lay the next tile on the other side of the line, butting against the first one (3). Form a square with two more tiles. Lay tiles around the square to form a pyramid (4). Continue in this way to fill one half of the room, remove the batten and tile the other half.

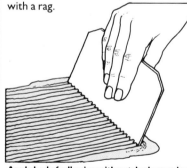

1 Peel off paper backing from adhesive tiles

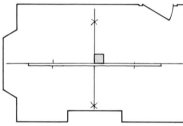

2 Place first tile in angle of intersecting lines

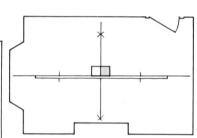

3 Butt up next tile on other side of line

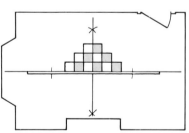

4 Lay tiles in a pyramid then fill in half room

GLUING VINYL TILES

Spread adhesive thinly but evenly across the floor, using a notched spreader, to stick about two or three tiles only. Lay the tiles carefully and wipe off surplus adhesive that's squeezed out with a rag.

Apply bed of adhesive with notched spreader

Single threshold bar

Finishing off the floor

As soon as you have laid all the floor tiles, wash over the surface with a damp cloth to remove any finger marks. It is not often necessary to polish vinyl tiles, but you can apply an emulsion floor polish if you wish.

Fit a straight metal strip (available from carpet suppliers) over the edge of the tiles when you finish at a doorway. When the tiles butt up to an area of carpet, fit a single threshold bar onto the edge of the carpeting (See left).

CUTTING TILES TO FIT

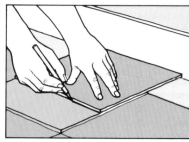

Trimming border tiles

Edges are rarely square, so cut border tiles to the skirting profile. To make a border tile, lay a loose one exactly on top of the last full tile. Place another tile on top but with its edge touching the wall. Draw along the edge of this tile with a pencil to mark the tile below. Remove the marked tile and cut along the line, then fit the cut off portion of the tile into the border.

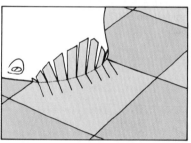

Cutting irregular shapes

To fit curves and mouldings, make a template for each tile out of thin card. Cut fingers which can be pressed against the object to reproduce its shape. Transfer the template to a tile and cut it out. You can also use a profile gauge to mark tiles for cutting complex curves.

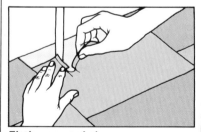

Fitting around pipes

Mark the position of the pipe on the tile using a compass. Draw parallel lines to the edge of the tile, taken from the perimeter of the circle. Measure halfway between the lines and cut a straight slit to the edge of the tile. Fold back the slit and slide the tile in place.

LAYING OTHER TYPES OF SOFT FLOOR TILES

Carpet tiles

Carpet tiles are laid as for vinyl tiles, except that they are not usually glued down. Set out centre lines on the floor (▷) but don't fit a guide batten: simply aligning the row of tiles with the marked lines is sufficient.

Carpet tiles have a pile which must be laid in the correct direction, sometimes indicated by arrows on the back face. One problem with loose-laid carpet tiles is preventing them from slipping – particularly noticeable in a large room.

Some tiles have ridges of rubber on the back which mean they will slip easily in one direction but not in another. The non-slip direction is typically denoted by an arrow on the back of the tile. It's usual to lay the tiles in pairs so that one prevents the other from moving.

Stick down every third row of tiles using double-sided carpet tape to make sure the tiles don't slide.

Cut and fit carpet tiles as described for vinyl tiles.

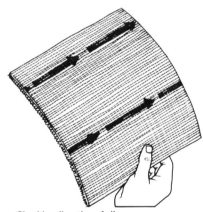

Checking direction of pile
Some carpet tiles have arrows on their back to indicate laying direction.

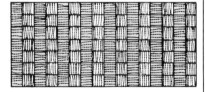

Using pile for decoration
Two typical arrangements of tiles using the pile to make decorative textures.

Cork tiles

Use the methods described for laying vinyl tiles to cut and fit cork tiles, but use a contact adhesive: thixotropic types allow a degree of movement as you position the tiles.

Make sure the tiles are level by tapping down the edges with a block of wood. Unfinished tiles can be sanded lightly to remove minor irregularities.

Vacuum then seal unfinished tiles with three or four coats of clear polyurethane varnish.

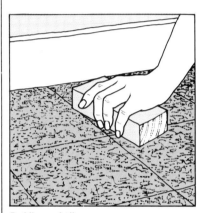

Bedding cork tiles
Bed the edges of cork tiles with a wood block.

Rubber tiles

Use the same methods for laying rubber tiles as for vinyl types. Use a latex flooring adhesive.

Laying rubber tiles
Lay large rubber tiles by placing one edge and corner against neighbouring tiles before lowering it onto a bed of adhesive.

NEAT DETAILING FOR SOFT FLOOR TILES

Covering a plinth

Create the impression of a floating bath panel or kitchen base units by running floor tiles up the face of the plinth. Hold carpet tiles into a tight bend with gripper strip (**1**) or glue other tiles in place for a similar detail. Glue a plastic moulding, normally used to seal around the edge of a bath, behind the floor covering to produce a curved detail which makes cleaning the floor a lot easier (**2**).

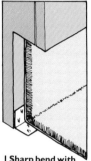

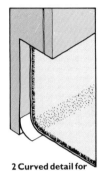

1 Sharp bend with gripper strip

2 Curved detail for easy cleaning

Cutting holes for pipes

With most soft floor tiles you can cut neat holes for central heating pipes using a home-made punch: cut a 150mm (6in) length of the same diameter pipe and sharpen the rim on the inside at one end with a metalworking file. Plot the position for the hole on the tile then place the punching tool on top. Hit the other end of the punch with a hammer to cut through the tile cleanly. With some carpet tiles you may have to cut round the backing to release the cut-out and prevent fraying with tape.

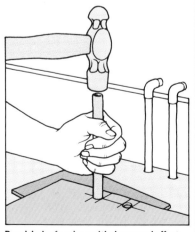

Punch holes for pipes with sharpened offcut

● **Access to plumbing**
If you are covering completely a bath panel with tiles, remember to make a lift-off section in the panel to gain access to pipes and taps around the bath.

LAYING CERAMIC FLOOR TILES

Ceramic floor tiles make a durable, hard surface that can also be extremely decorative. Laying the tiles on a floor is similar to hanging them on a wall, *although being somewhat thicker than wall tiles, you have to be especially careful when cutting them to fit for neat and accurate results.*

● **Battens on concrete**
Use masonry nails to hold battens onto a concrete floor.

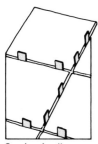

Spacing the tiles
Use offcuts of thick card to set ceramic floor tiles apart consistently to allow for grouting.

● **Grouting the joins**
Grout the tiles as for walls, but fill the joins flush rather than indenting them, so that dirt will not clog them. A dark grout is less likely to show up dirt.

Setting out for tiling
Mark out the floor as for soft floor tiles then set out the field with battens.
1 Fix temporary guide battens at the edge of the field on two adjacent walls farthest from the door
2 Ensure that the battens are at true right-angles by measuring the diagonal
3 Dry-lay a square of 16 tiles in the angle as a final check

Setting out

You cannot lay ceramic tiles on a suspended wooden floor without covering it with 12mm (½in) plywood screwed down every 300mm (1ft). A flat, dry concrete floor is ideal.

Mark out the floor as for soft floor tiles (◁) and work out the spacing to achieve even, fairly wide border tiles. Nail two softwood guide battens to the floor, aligned with the last row of whole tiles on two adjacent walls farthest from

the door. Set the battens at a right-angle – even a small error will become obvious by the time you reach the other end of the room. Check the angle by measuring three units from one corner along one batten and four units along the other. Measure the diagonal between the marks: it should measure five units if the battens form an angle of 90 degrees. Make a final check by dry-laying a square of tiles in the angle.

Laying the tiles

Use a proprietary floor tile adhesive that is waterproof and slightly flexible when set. Spread it on using a plain or notched trowel, according to the manufacturer's recommendations. The normal procedure is to apply adhesive to the floor for the main area of tiling but to butter the back of individual cut tiles as well.

Spread enough adhesive on the floor for about sixteen tiles. Press the tiles into the adhesive, starting in the corner. Work along both battens then fill in between, to form the square. Few floor tiles have spacing lugs, so use plastic spacers or card.

Check the alignment of the tiles with a straightedge and make sure they're lying flat by spanning them with a spirit level. Work along one batten laying squares of sixteen tiles each time. Tile the rest of the floor in the same way, working back towards the door. Leave

the floor for 24 hours before you walk on it to remove the guide battens and fit the border tiles.

Cutting ceramic floor tiles
Measure and cut the tiles to fit the border as described for wall tiles (◁). Because they are thicker, floor tiles will not snap quite so easily, so if you have a large area to fill, buy or hire a tile cutting jig.

Alternatively, make your own device by nailing two scraps of 12mm (½in) thick plywood to 50 × 25mm (2 × 1in) softwood battens, leaving a parallel gap between them which is just wide enough to take a tile. Hold the device on edge, insert a scored tile into the gap, up to the scored line – which should be uppermost – and press down on the free end (see below right). Snap thin strips from the edge in this way. Saw or nibble curved shapes (◁).

LAYING MOSAIC FLOOR TILES

Set out mosaic tiles on a floor as for ceramic floor tiles. Spread on the adhesive then lay the tiles, paper facing uppermost, with spacers that match the gaps between individual pieces. Press the sheets into the adhesive, using a block of wood to tamp them level. Remove the spacers and soak then peel off the facing with warm water 24 hours later. Grout as normal.

If you have to fit a sheet of mosaic tiles around an obstruction remove individual mosaic pieces as close to the profile as possible. Fit the sheet (**1**) then cut and replace the pieces to fit around the shapes.

If you're using mosaics in areas of heavy traffic – a step on the patio, for example – protect vulnerable edges with a nosing of ordinary ceramic floor tiles to match or contrast (**2**).

1 Remove mosaic pieces to fit around pipe

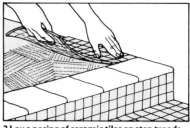

2 Lay a nosing of ceramic tiles on step treads

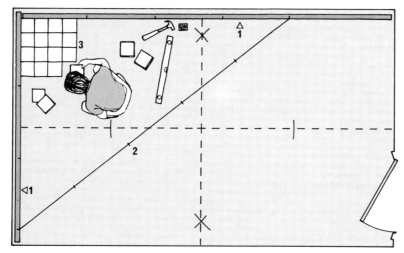

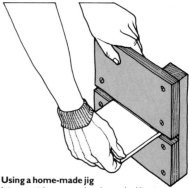

Using a home-made jig
It is essential to ensure that the marked line is positioned parallel to the edge of the plywood or the tile will not snap accurately.

LAYING QUARRY TILES

Quarry tiles are the best choice for a tough, hardwearing flooring that will receive a lot of heavy foot traffic. But beware: they're fairly thick and making even a straight cut is not easy. Reserve them for areas that don't require a lot of complex shaping.

Don't lay quarry tiles on a suspended wooden floor; replace the floorboards

with 18 or 22mm (¾ or 1in) exterior-grade plywood to provide a sufficiently flat and rigid base. A concrete floor presents no problems, providing it is free from damp. So long as the floor is reasonably flat, the mortar bed on which the tiles are laid will take care of the fine levelling.

CUTTING QUARRY TILES

Because quarry tiles are difficult to cut you may think it worthwhile having them cut by a specialist tile supplier. Measure border tiles as described for wall tiles then, having scored the line, number each one on the bottom and mark the waste with a felt-tip pen.

If you want to cut the tiles yourself, scribe them with a tile cutter, then make a shallow cut down each edge with a saw file (▷). With the face side of the tile held in a gloved hand, strike behind the scored line with the cross pein of a hammer.

SEE ALSO
Details for: ▷
Saw file   77

Setting out for tiling

Set out two guide battens in a corner of the room at right-angles to each other, as described for ceramic floor tiles, opposite. The depth of the battens should measure about twice the thickness of the tiles to allow for the mortar bed. Fix them temporarily to a concrete floor with long masonry nails. The level of the battens is essential, so check with a spirit level; pack out under

the battens with scraps of hardboard or card where necessary. Mark tile widths along each batten, leaving 3mm (⅛in) gaps between for grouting, as a guide to positioning.

Dry-lay a square of sixteen tiles in the angle, then nail a third batten to the floor, butting the tiles and parallel with one of the other battens. Level and mark it as before.

Bedding down the tiles

Quarry tiles are laid on a bed of mortar mixed from 1 part cement: 3 parts builder's sand. When water is added, the mortar should be stiff enough to hold an impression when squeezed in your hand.

Soak quarry tiles in water prior to laying to prevent them sucking water from the mortar too rapidly, when a poor bond could result. Cut a stout board to span the parallel battens: this will be used to level the mortar bed and tiles. Cut a notch in each end to fit between the battens, and the thickness of a tile less 3mm (⅛in).

Spread the mortar to a depth of about 12mm (½in) to cover the area of sixteen tiles. Level it by dragging the notched side of the board across.

Dust dry cement on the mortar to

provide a good key for the tiles, then lay the tiles along three sides of the square against the battens. Fill in the square, spacing the tiles equally by adjusting them with a trowel.

Tamp down the tiles gently with the un-notched side of the board until they are level with the battens. If the mortar is too stiff, brush water into the joins. Wipe mortar from the faces of the tiles before it hardens, or it will stain.

Fill in between the battens then move one batten back to form another bay of the same dimension. Level it with the first section of tiles. Tile section-by-section until the main floor is complete. When the floor is hard enough to walk on, lift the battens and fill in the border tiles.

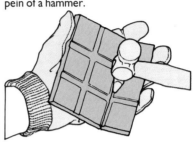

Score tile face: tap the back with a hammer

Levelling the mortar
With a notch located over each guide batten, drag the levelling board towards you.

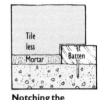

Notching the levelling board
Cut the same notch at each end of the board for levelling the mortar.

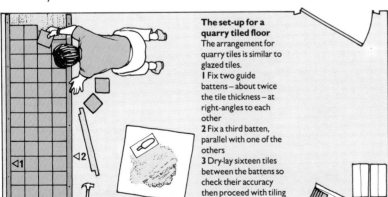

The set-up for a quarry tiled floor
The arrangement for quarry tiles is similar to glazed tiles.
1 Fix two guide battens – about twice the tile thickness – at right-angles to each other
2 Fix a third batten, parallel with one of the others
3 Dry-lay sixteen tiles between the battens so check their accuracy then proceed with tiling

Levelling border tiles
Use a notched piece of plywood to level the mortar in the margin and tamp down the tiles with a block.

• **Finishing off the quarry tiling**
Grout quarry tiles as for ceramic floor tiles, using cement or proprietary waterproof grout. Clean it off the surface by sprinkling sawdust onto it and wiping off with a cloth. Wash the finished floor with a soapless detergent.

LAYING SHEET VINYL

Vinyl floorcovering makes a durable, wall-to-wall surface for floors subject to likely spillages of water, such as the kitchen, utility room and bathroom.

There are numerous colours, patterns and embossed effects available, and you will find most types straightforward to lay if you follow a systematic routine.

Leave the vinyl in a room for 24 to 48 hours before laying, preferably opened flat or at least stood on end, loosely rolled. Assuming there are no seams, start by fitting the longest wall first. Drive a nail through a wooden lath about 50mm (2in) from one end.

Pull the vinyl away from the wall by approximately 35mm (1½in). Make sure it is parallel with the wall or the main axis of the room. Use the nailed strip to scribe a line following the skirting (**1**). Cut along the vinyl with a sharp knife or scissors and slide the sheet up against the wall.

To get the rest of the sheet to lie as flat as possible, cut a triangular notch out of each corner. Make a straight cut down to the floor at external corners. Remove as much waste as possible leaving 50 to 75mm (2 to 3in) turned up all round.

Press the vinyl into the angle between skirting and floor with a bolster. Align a metal straightedge with the crease and run along it with a sharp knife held at a slight angle to the skirting (**2**). If your trimming is less than perfect, nail a cover strip of quadrant moulding to the skirting.

1 Fit to first wall by scribing with a nailed strip

Trimming and gluing vinyl sheet

Trimming to fit a doorway
Work around the door frame moulding making straight cuts and removing triangular notches at each change of angle as if they were miniature corners. Crease the vinyl against the floor and trim the waste. Make a straight cut across the opening and fit a threshold bar over the edge of the sheet.

Cutting around an obstruction
To fit around a WC pan or basin pedestal, fold back the sheet and pierce it with a knife just above floor level. Draw the blade up towards the edge. Make triangular cuts around the base, gradually working around the curve until the sheet can lie flat on the floor (**3**). Crease and cut off the waste.

Sticking the sheet
Modern vinyls can be loose-laid, but you may prefer to glue the edges and especially along a door opening. Peel back the edge and spread a band of the recommended flooring adhesive with a toothed spreader (**4**) or use a 50mm (2in) wide double-sided tape.

Making a join
If you have to join widths of vinyl, scribe one edge as described above, then overlap the free edge with the second sheet until the pattern matches exactly. Cut through both pieces with a knife, then remove the waste strips.

Without moving the sheets, fold back both cut edges, apply tape or adhesive and press the join together.

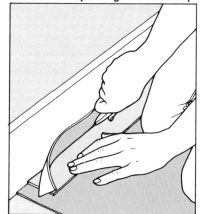
2 Press the edge to the skirting and cut

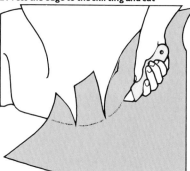
3 Make triangular cuts around a curve

Positioning the vinyl
Aligning the vinyl sheet squarely on the floor is essential.
1 Fit the longest, uninterrupted wall
2 Cut triangular notches at each external and internal corner so the sheet will lie flat
3 Allow folds of about 75mm (3in) all round for scribing to fit accurately
4 Make a straight cut against the door opening so a threshold bar can be fixed

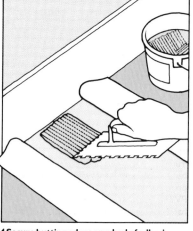
4 Secure butting edges on a bed of adhesive

DECORATOR'S TOOL KIT

Most of us decorate our own houses or flats to some extent, and decorators' tools are fairly common. Though traditionalists will stick to tried and tested tools and materials of proven reliability others will prefer recent innovations aimed at making the work easier and faster for the home decorator.

TOOLS FOR PREPARATION

Whether you are painting papering or tiling, the surface to which the materials will be applied must be sound and clean.

Straight scraper

Serrated scraper

Wallpaper or paint scraper
The wide stiff blade of a scraper is for removing softened paint or soaked wallpaper. The best scrapers have high-quality steel blades and riveted rosewood handles. One with a 100 to 125mm (4 to 5in) wide blade is best for stripping wallpaper, but a narrow one, no more than 25mm (1in) wide, is useful for removing paint from window or door frames. A serrated scraper will score impervious wallcovering so that water or stripping solution can penetrate it faster. If you use one, try not to damage the wall behind the covering.

Vinyl gloves
Most people wear ordinary 'rubber' gloves to protect their hands when washing down or preparing paintwork, but tough PVC work gloves are more hardwearing and will protect you from a great many harmful chemicals.

ACQUIRING TOOLS

It will not cost you a fortune to buy a reasonable kit of good-quality decorating tools and you can hire some of the more specialized equipment which you will use only occasionally.

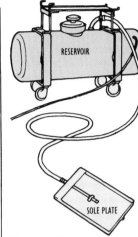

RESERVOIR

SOLE PLATE

Steam wallpaper stripper
To remove wallpaper quickly, especially thick wallcovering, hire an electric steam-generating stripper. All such strippers work on the same principle, but follow any specific safety instructions that come with the machine.

Using a steam stripper
Fill its reservoir and plug it into a socket outlet 15 minutes before starting work so as to generate a good head of steam. Hold the steaming plate against the wallpaper until it is soft enough to be removed with a scraper. The time for this will depend on the type of the wallcovering.

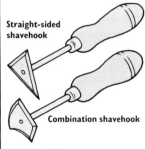

Straight-sided shavehook

Combination shavehook

Shavehook
This is a special scraper for removing old paint and varnish. A straight-sided triangular one is fine for flat surfaces but one with a combination blade can also be used on concave and convex mouldings. You pull a shavehook towards you to remove the softened paint.

Hot air stripper
The gas blowtorch was once the professional's tool for softening old paint so as to strip it, but the modern electric hot air stripper is much easier to use. It is as efficient as a blowtorch but involves little risk of scorching woodwork. Early models were heavy and tiring to use, but today's are light enough to be used for long periods without fatigue. On some strippers the air temperature can be adjusted. Others have interchangeable nozzles shaped to concentrate the heated air or direct it away from glass panes.

Filling knife
A filling knife looks like a paint scraper but has a flexible blade for forcing filler into cracks in timber or plaster. Patch large areas of damaged wall with a plasterer's trowel (▷).

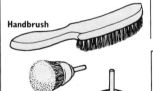

Handbrush

Cup brush

Wire brushes
A handbrush with steel wire 'bristles' will remove flaking paint and rust particles from metalwork before repainting. The job is easier with a rotary wire cup brush in a power drill, but wear goggles or safety glasses if you use one.

Mastic guns
Non-setting (permanently flexible) mastic is for sealing gaps between masonry and wooden frames and other joints between materials whose different rates of expansion will eventually crack and eject a rigid filler. You can buy mastic that is squeezed direct from its plastic tube like toothpaste, but it is easier to apply from a cartridge in a spring-loaded gun or an aerosol can with a special nozzle.

Tacky rag
Though you may find it hard to get one, a resin-impregnated cloth called a 'tacky rag' is ideal for picking up particles of dust and hard paint from a surface prepared for painting. Failing a tacky rag use a lint-free cloth dampened with white spirit.

Dusting brush
A dusting brush has long soft bristles for clearing dust out of mouldings and crevices just before painting woodwork. You can use an ordinary paintbrush if you keep it clean and reserve it for the job.

WET AND DRY PAPER

Wet and dry abrasive paper is for smoothing new paintwork or varnish before applying the final coat. It is a waterproof backing paper with silicon carbide particles glued to it. Dip a piece in water and rub the paintwork until a slurry of paint and water forms. Wipe it off with a cloth before it dries, then rinse the paper clean and continue.

● **Essential tools**
Wallpaper scraper
Combination spokeshave
Filling knife
Hot air stripper
Wire brush

PAINTBRUSHES

Some paintbrushes are made from natural animal hair. Hog bristle is the best, but it is often mixed with inferior horsehair or oxhair to reduce cost. Synthetic bristle brushes are usually the least expensive, and are quite adequate for the home decorator.

Paint kettle
To carry paint to a worksite decant a little into a cheap, lightweight plastic paint kettle.

Bristle types
Bristle is ideal for paintbrushes because each hair tapers naturally and splits at the tip into even finer filaments that hold paint well. Bristle is also tough and resilient. Synthetic 'bristle', usually of nylon, is made to resemble the characteristics of real bristle, and a good-quality nylon brush will serve the average painter as well as a bristle one.

Choosing a brush
The bristles of a good brush – the 'filling' – are densely packed. When you fan them with your fingers they should spring back into shape immediately. Flex the tip of the brush against your hand to see if any bristles work loose. Even a good brush will shed a few individual ones at first, but never clumps. The ferrule should be fixed firmly to the handle.

12mm (½in)   25mm (1in)   50mm (2in)

● **Essential tools**
Flat brushes 12, 25 and 50mm (½, 1 and 2in)
Wallbrush 150mm (6in)

Flat paintbrush
The filling is set in rubber–or occasionally in pitch or resin–and bound to the wooden or plastic handle by a pressed-metal ferrule. You will need several sizes up to 50mm (2in) for painting, varnishing and staining woodwork.

One-knot paintbrush
The bristles of a one-knot paintbrush are bound to a cylindrical handle with string, wire or a metal ferrule. Their grouping makes them very resilient, but when flexed against a surface they will fan out like those of the commoner flat paintbrush.

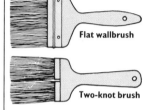

Flat wallbrush

Two-knot brush

Wallbrush
To apply emulsion paint by brush use a 150mm (6in) flat wallbrush or a two-knot brush of the kind favoured by continental painters and decorators.

Cutting-in brush
The filling of a cutting-in brush, or 'bevelled sash tool', is cut at an angle for painting moulded glazing bars right up into the corners and against the glass, though most painters make do with a 12mm (½in) flat brush.

STENCIL AND GRAIN-EFFECT TOOLS

Stencil brush
A stencil brush has short stiff bristles. The paint is stippled on with their tips and a cut-out template defines the painted shape.

Grainers
These are special brushes for reproducing the effects of natural woodgrain on paint or varnish. A 'mottler' has a dense soft filling of squirrel hair for lifting bands or streaks of colour to simulate figured hardwoods. A 'pencil grainer' has a row of fine brushes mounted in one handle for drawing patterns of parallel lines.

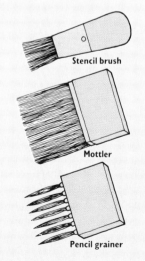

Stencil brush

Mottler

Pencil grainer

1 Wire radiator brush

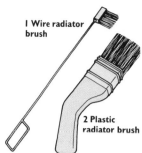

2 Plastic radiator brush

Radiator brush
Unless you take a radiator off the wall for decorating you need a special brush to paint the back of it and the wall behind it. There are two kinds: one with a standard flat paintbrush head at right angles to its long wire handle (**1**), the other like a conventional paintbrush but with a cranked plastic handle (**2**).

Banister brush
Use a household banister brush for painting rough or rendered walls.

Paint shield

Glass scraper

Paint shield and scraper
There are various plastic and metal shields for protecting glass when window frames and glazing bars are being painted, and glass that does get spattered can be cleaned with a razor blade clipped in a special holder.

CLEANING BRUSHES

● **Emulsion paint**
As soon as you finish working with emulsion paint wash it from the brush with warm soapy water, flexing the bristles between your fingers to work all paint out of the roots, then rinse the brush in clean water and shake out the excess. Smooth the bristles and slip an elastic band round their tips to hold the shape of the filling while it is drying.

Holding the shape of a brush

● **Oil paint**
If you are using oil paint you can suspend the brush overnight in enough water to cover the bristles, blot it with kitchen paper next day and continue painting.
When you have finished, brush excess paint out on newspaper, then flex the bristles in a bowl of thinners. Some finishes need special thinners, so check for this on the container; otherwise use white spirit or a chemical brush cleaner. Wash the dirty thinners from the brush with hot soapy water, then rinse it.

Soaking a brush

● **Hardened paint**
If paint has hardened on a brush, soak its bristles in brush cleaner to soften the paint which will become water-soluble and will wash out easily with hot water. If the old paint is unusually stubborn dip the bristles in some paint stripper (⬛).

STORING PAINTBRUSHES

For long-term storage fold soft paper over the filling and secure it with an elastic band round paper and ferrule.

PAINT PADS

Paint pads are a fairly recent development aimed at helping inexperienced painters to apply oil and emulsion paint quickly and evenly. They are not universally popular, but no one disputes their value in painting large flat areas. They cover quickly and are unlikely to drip paint if they are loaded properly.

Standard pads
There is a range of rectangular pads for painting walls, ceilings and flat woodwork. They have short mohair pile on their painting surfaces and handles on their backs.

Edging pad
To paint a straight edge—between a wall and a ceiling, for instance—use an edging pad with small wheels or rollers that guide it parallel to the adjacent surface.

Sash pad
A sash pad has a small mohair sole for painting glazing bars. Most sash pads have plastic guides on their backs to prevent them straying onto the glass.

PRESSURIZED PAINTING SYSTEM

With a pressurized painting system you can work continuously for as long as its reservoir contains paint. An ordinary soda-syphon bulb delivers the paint at a slow but steady pace, and a control button on the handle releases it to the painting head, which is detachable and can be a roller, a brush or a pad as required. You can carry the reservoir or clip it to your belt for greater freedom of movement.

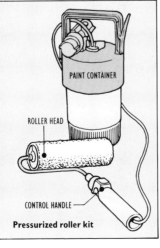

PAINT CONTAINER

ROLLER HEAD

CONTROL HANDLE

Pressurized roller kit

CLEANING PAINT PADS

Before dipping a new pad into paint, brush it with a clothes brush to remove any loose nylon filaments.

● When you finish painting, blot the pad on old newspaper, then wash it in the appropriate solvent—water for emulsion, white spirit or brush cleaner for oil paints, or any special thinners recommended by the paint manufacturer. Squeeze the foam and rub the pile with gloved fingertips, then wash the pad in hot soapy water and rinse it.

● Even after washing, a new pad may be stained by paint, but the colour will not contaminate the next batch of fresh paint.

Pad tray
Pads and trays are normally sold as sets, but if you buy a separate tray get one with a loading roller that distributes paint evenly onto the sole of a pad drawn across it.

PAINT ROLLERS

A paint roller is efficient for painting large areas quickly. On the better type the cylindrical sleeve that applies the paint slides onto a revolving sprung-wire cage on a cranked handle. The sleeves on this type of roller are easily changed. Don't buy one whose sleeve is held in place by a small nut and washer. Even if the nut doesn't get lost, corroded or paint-clogged it's much too fiddly.

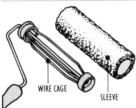

WIRE CAGE   SLEEVE

Sizes of roller sleeves
Sleeves for standard rollers range from 175mm (7in) to about 337mm (1ft 1½in) in length but there are smaller rollers for painting narrow strips of wall or woodwork.

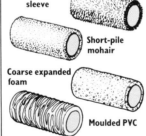

Deep-pile sleeve

Short-pile mohair

Coarse expanded foam

Moulded PVC

Types of roller sleeves
There are roller sleeves of various materials to suit different paints and surface textures. Most are of **sheepskin** or **synthetic fibre,** both of which suit emulsion paint and leave an even finely textured finish. Use a **deep-pile** sleeve to paint a heavily textured surface, a **medium-pile** one for smooth walls and ceilings.

Short-pile roller sleeves, usually of mohair, are made for use with oil paints.

The cheap **plastic-foam** sleeves are unsatisfactory both with oil and emulsion paints. They leave tiny air bubbles in the painted surface and the foam often distorts as it dries after washing. But they are cheap enough to be thrown away after use with finishes—like bituminous paint—which would be hard to remove even from a short-pile roller sleeve.

Use a **coarse expanded-foam** sleeve for applying textured coatings. There are also **moulded PVC** rollers with embossed surfaces to pattern all kinds of textured paints and coatings.

Extending a roller
If your roller has a hollow handle you can plug it onto a telescopic extension handle so as to reach a ceiling from the floor. Loading an extended roller can be tricky, but you can buy one with a built-in reservoir that keeps the roller charged and holds enough paint for a large area.

CLEANING A ROLLER

Remove most of the excess paint by running the roller back and forth across old newspaper. If you plan to use the roller next day apply a few drops of the appropriate thinners to the sleeve and wrap it in plastic. Otherwise clean, wash and rinse the sleeve before the paint can set.

● **Emulsion paint**
If you've been using emulsion paint flush most of it out under running water, then massage a little liquid detergent into the pile and flush it again.

● **Roller washer**
You can mechanize the job with a roller washer that stands in the sink, its hose attached to a tap. Lower the roller, complete with sleeve, into the washer and turn on the tap. The force of the water spins the roller head and flushes the paint from it out of the base of the washer into the drain. The roller is cleaned in about one or two minutes.

● **Oil paint**
To remove oil paint pour some thinners into the roller tray and slowly roll the sleeve back and forth in it. Squeeze the roller and agitate the pile with your fingertips. When the paint has all dissolved wash the sleeve in hot soapy water.

2   3

1 Corner roller
You cannot paint into a corner with a standard roller, so unless there are to be different adjacent colours, paint the corner first with a shaped corner roller.
2 Pipe roller
A pipe roller has two narrow sleeves, mounted side by side, which locate over the cylindrical pipework to paint it.
3 Radiator roller
This is a thin roller on a long wire handle for painting behind radiators and pipes.

Roller tray
A paint roller is loaded from a sloping plastic or metal tray whose deep end acts as a paint reservoir. Load the roller by rolling paint from the deep end up and down the tray's ribbed slope once or twice so as to get even distribution on the sleeve.

● **Essential tools**
Standard pads
50 and 200mm
(2 and 8in)
Sash pad
Large roller and selection of sleeves
Roller tray

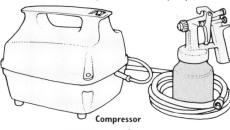

Spraying textured paint
Hire a special gravity-fed spray gun to apply reinforced emulsions and 'tyrolean' finishes. The material is loaded into a hopper on top of the gun.

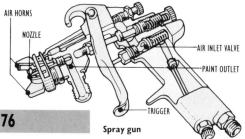

Compressor

AIR HORNS

NOZZLE

AIR INLET VALVE

PAINT OUTLET

TRIGGER

Spray gun

PAINTSPRAYING EQUIPMENT

Spraying is so fast and efficient that it's worth considering if you plan to paint the outside walls of a building. The equipment is expensive to buy but it can be hired from most tool-hire outlets. You can spray most exterior paints and finishes if they are thinned properly but tell the hire company which one you wish to use so that they can supply the right spray gun with the correct nozzle. Hire goggles and a facemask at the same time.

Preparation
As far as possible plan to work on a dry and windless day, and allow time to mask off windows, doors and pipework. Follow the setting-up and handling instructions supplied with the equipment, and if you are new to the work, practise a little beforehand on an inconspicuous section of wall.

Compressor-operated spray
With this equipment the paint is mixed with pressurized air to emerge as a fine spray. Some compressors deliver compressed air to an intermediate tank and top it up as air is drawn off by the spray gun, but most hired ones supply air directly to the gun. The trigger opens a valve to admit air, at the same time opening the paint outlet at the nozzle. The paint is drawn from a container, usually mounted below the gun, and mixes with compressed air at the tip. Most guns have air-delivery horns at the sides of the nozzle to produce a fan-shaped pattern.

Airless sprayer
In an airless sprayer an electric pump delivers the paint itself at high pressure to the spray gun. The paint is picked up through a tube inserted in the paint container and the pump forces it through a high-pressure hose to a filter and pressure regulator which is adjustable to produce required spray patterns. The paint leaves the nozzle at such high pressure that it can penetrate skin, so most such spray guns have safety shields on their nozzles.

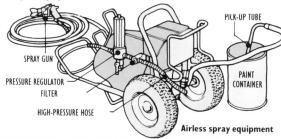

SPRAY GUN

PRESSURE REGULATOR FILTER

HIGH-PRESSURE HOSE

PICK-UP TUBE

PAINT CONTAINER

Airless spray equipment

Follow any safety advice supplied with the sprayer but take the following precautions in any case:

● **Wear goggles and a facemask when spraying.**
● **Don't spray indoors without proper extraction equipment.**
● **Atomised oil paint is highly flammable, so have no naked lights and do not smoke when you spray.**
● **Never leave the equipment unattended, especially where there are children or pets; if the gun has a safety lock, engage it while you are not actually spraying.**
● **Unplug the equipment and release the pressure in the hose before trying to clear a blocked nozzle.**
● **Never aim the gun at yourself or anyone else. If you accidentally spray your skin at close quarters with an airless gun seek medical advice at once.**

CLEANING A SPRAY GUN

Empty out any paint left in the container and add some thinners. Spray the thinners until it emerges clear, then release the pressure and dismantle the spray nozzle. Clean the parts with a solvent-dampened rag and wipe out the container.

COMMON SPRAYING FAULTS

Streaked paintwork
An uneven streaked finish results if you don't overlap the passes of the gun.

Patchy paintwork
Coverage won't be consistent if you move the gun in an arc. Keep it pointing directly at the wall and moving parallel to it.

Orange-peel texture
A wrinkle paint film resembling the texture of orange peel is usually caused by spraying paint that is too thick, but if the paint seems to be of the right consistency you may be moving the spray gun too slowly.

Runs
Runs will occur if you apply too much paint, probably through holding the gun too close to the surface you're spraying.

Powdery finish
This is caused by paint drying before it reaches the wall. Hold the gun a little closer to the wall surface.

Spattering
Pressure that's too high will produce a speckled finish. Lower the pressure until the finish becomes satisfactory.

Spitting
A partly clogged nozzle will make the gun splutter. Clear the nozzle with a stiff bristle from a brush—never use wire—then wipe it with a rag dampened in thinners.

PAPERHANGERS' TOOLS

You can improvise some of the tools needed for paperhanging, but even purpose-made equipment is inexpensive so it's worth having a proper kit.

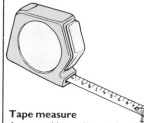

Tape measure
A retractable steel tape is best for measuring walls and ceilings to estimate the amount of wallcovering you'll need.

Plumb bob and line

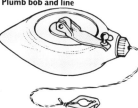

Retractable plumb line

Plumb line
Any small weight suspended on fine string can be used to mark the position of one edge of a strip of wallpaper. Hold the end of the line near the ceiling, allow the weight to come to rest, then mark the wall at points down the length of the line.

A purpose-made plumb line has a pointed metal weight called a plumb bob. In expensive versions the line retracts into a hollow plumb bob containing coloured chalk and is coated with chalk as it is withdrawn. When the line hangs vertically stretch it taut, then snap it against the wall like a bowstring to leave a chalked line.

Paste brush
Apply paste to the back of wallcovering with a wide wallbrush (◁). Alternatively use a short-pile mohair roller. Clean either tool by washing it in warm water.

PASTING TABLE

Though you can paste wallcoverings on any convenient flat surface a proper pasting table is ideal. It stands higher than the average dining table and is only 25mm (1in) wider than a standard roll of wallpaper, making it easier to apply paste without spreading onto the work surface. The underframe folds flat and the top is hinged, so the table can be carried from room to room and stowed in a small space.

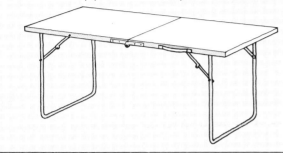

Paperhanger's brush
This is a brush used for smoothing wallcovering onto a surface. Its bristles should be soft, so as not to damage delicate paper, but springy enough to provide the pressure to squeeze excess paste and air bubbles from beneath the wallcovering. Wash the brush in warm water when you finish work to prevent paste hardening on the tips of the bristles.

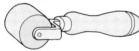

Seam roller
Use a hardwood or plastic seam roller to press down butted joints between adjacent strips of wallpaper, but not on embossed or delicate wallcoverings.

Rubber   Felt

Smoothing roller
There are rubber rollers for squeezing trapped air from under wallcoverings, but use a felt one on delicate and flocked wallpapers.

Paperhanger's scissors
Any fairly large scissors can be used for trimming wallpaper to length, but proper paperhanger's scissors have extra-long blades to achieve a straight cut.

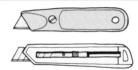

Craft knife
Use a knife to trim paper round light fittings and switches and to achieve perfect butt joints by cutting through overlapping edges of paper. The knife must be extremely sharp to avoid tearing the paper. so use one with disposable blades that you can change easily when one gets blunt. Some craft knives have short double-ended blades clamped in a metal or plastic handle. Others have long retractable blades that can be snapped off in short sections to leave a new sharp point.

TILING TOOLS

Most of the tools in a tiler's kit are for applying ceramic wall and floor tiles, but others are needed for laying soft tiles and vinyl sheeting.

Spirit level
You will need a spirit level for setting up temporary battens to align a field of tiles both horizontally and vertically.

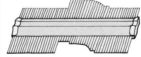

Profile gauge
A profile gauge is for copying the shapes of pipework or door mouldings to provide a pattern for fitting soft floorcoverings. As you press the steel pins of the gauge against the object you wish to copy they slide back, mirroring the shape. When you want to copy another shape press the needles against a flat surface to reposition them in a straight line.

Serrated trowel
Make a ridged bed of adhesive for ceramic tiles by drawing the toothed edge of a plastic or steel tiler's trowel through the material.

Tile cutter
A tile cutter is a square-section rod of steel with a pointed tungsten-carbide tip. The tip is for scoring the glazed surface of a ceramic tile so that it will snap cleanly along the scored line. Other cutters have steel wheels like glass cutters.

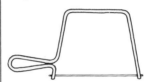

Saw file
A saw file has a bent metal frame that holds the thin wire rod under tension. The rod is coated with particles of tungsten-carbide hard enough to cut through ceramic tiles. Circular in section, the file will cut in any direction, so it can cut curved and straight lines with equal ease.

Squeegee
A squeegee has a blade of hard rubber mounted in a wooden handle. Use one for spreading grout into the gaps between ceramic tiles.

Nibblers
It is impossible to snap a very narrow strip off a ceramic tile. Instead score the line with a tile cutter, then break off the waste little by little with tile nibblers. They resemble pincers but have sharper jaws of tungsten-carbide that open automatically when you relax your grip on the spring-loaded handles.

TILE-CUTTING JIGS

A tile-cutting jig greatly simplifies the cutting and fitting of border tiles to fill the edges of a field of tiles. With the one tool you can measure the gap, score the tile and snap it along the scored line.

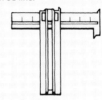

Using the jig
To measure the size of the tile to be cut slide the jig open until one pointer is against the adjacent wall and the other is against the edge of the last full tile (1). The jig automatically allows for grouting.

Fit the jig over the tile to be cut and with the tile cutter score the tile through the slot in the jig (2).

The cutter includes a pair of clippers with angled jaws for snapping the tile in two. Align the scored line with the pointer on the jaws and squeeze the handles until the tile breaks cleanly (3).

1 Measure the margin

2 Score the tile

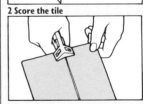

3 Snap the tile

Floor tile jig
Large cutting jigs for floor tiles can be hired or bought from good DIY stockists.

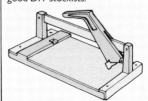

Staple gun
A staple gun is used for fixing mineral-fibre tiles to battens attached to a ceiling. The hand-operated type has a trigger that works a spring-loaded striker, which drives two-pronged staples into the work. It can be tiring to use with an outstretched arm. An electronic tacker makes light work of the largest ceilings and is much more powerful than the hand-operated tool, though its force is adjustable to suit the various materials.

Hand-operated gun

Electronic tacker

● **Essential tools**
Steel tape measure
Plumb line
Paste brush
Paperhanger's brush
Seam roller
Scissors
Craft knife
Pasting table
Spirit level
Serrated trowel
Tile cutter and jig
Nibblers
Saw file
Squeegee

GLOSSARY OF TERMS

Aggregate
Particles of sand added to paint to make a textured finish.

Architrave
The moulding around a door or window.

Arris
The sharp edge at the meeting of two surfaces.

Baluster
One of a set of posts supporting a stair handrail.

Balustrade
The protective barrier alongside a staircase or landing.

Bannister
See balustrade and baluster.

Batten
A narrow strip of wood.

Blind
To cover with sand.

Blown
To have broken away, as when a layer of cement rendering has parted from a wall.

Consumer unit
A box containing the house electrical-circuit fuses or miniature circuit breakers. A consumer unit is fitted with a master switch that turns off the supply of electricity to the whole building.

Cornice
The continuous horizontal moulding between the walls and ceiling.

Coving
A pre-fabricated moulding used to make a cornice.

Dado
The lower part of an interior wall – usually defined with a moulded rail.

Drop
A strip of wallpaper cut to length ready for pasting to a wall.

Efflorescence
A white powdery deposit caused by soluble salts migrating to the surface of a wall or ceiling.

End grain
The surface of wood exposed after cutting across the fibres.

Fascia board
The strip of wood that covers the ends of rafters and to which external guttering is fixed.

Feather
To wear away or smooth an edge until it is undetectable.

Galvanized
Covered with a protective coating of zinc.

Gel
A substance with a thick jelly-like consistency.

Grain
The general direction of wood fibres. *or* The pattern produced on the surface of timber by cutting through the fibres.

Hardwood
Timber cut from deciduous trees.

Header face
The end of a house brick.

Key
To abrade or incise a surface to provide a better grip when gluing something to it or painting over it.

Knotting
A shellac-based sealer used to prevent softwood resin bleeding through a coat of paint.

Lath and plaster
A method of finishing a timber-framed wall or ceiling. Narrow strips of wood are nailed to the wall studs or joists to provide a supporting framework for the plaster.

Mastic
A commercially prepared non-setting compound used to seal joints.

Microporous
Used to describe a finish which allows timber to dry out while protecting it from rainwater.

Muntin
A central vertical member of a panel door.

Oxidize
To form a layer of metal oxide as in rusting.

Papier mâché
A stiff filler made by mashing newsprint (newspaper) in warm water mixed with wallpaper paste.

Plasterboard
A wallcladding material comprising a core of aerated gypsum plaster covered on both sides with a strong paper lining.

Primary colours
The three pure colours – red, blue and yellow.

Primer
The first coat of a paint system. It protects the workpiece and reduces absorption of subsequent coats.

Profile
The outline or contour of an object.

Riser
The vertical part of a step.

Rubber
A pad of cotton wool wrapped in soft cloth used to apply stain, shellac polish etc.

Running bond
The pattern formed by bricks laid with their vertical joints staggered regularly. Also known as stretcher bond.

Scribe
To copy the profile of a surface on the edge of sheet material which is to be butted against it. *or* To mark a line with a pointed tool.

Shellac
A substance exuded by the lac insect. It is dissolved in industrial alcohol to make French polish.

Slipstone
A small teardrop-section sharpening stone used to hone the cutting edges of woodworking gouges.

Softwood
Timber cut from coniferous trees.

Stile
A vertical member of a door, window sash or ladder.

Stopper
A wood filler which matches the colour of the timber.

Stretcher face
The long face of a house brick.

String
A board which runs from one floor level to another and into which staircase treads and risers are jointed. The one on the open side of a staircase is an open string, the one against the wall is a wall string.

Stud partition
An interior timber-framed dividing wall.

Studs
The vertical members of a timber-framed wall.

Template
A cut-out pattern to help shape a workpiece accurately.

Thinners
A solvent used to dilute paint or varnish.

Thixotropic
A property of some paints which have a jelly-like consistency until stirred or applied, at which point they become liquid.

Top coat
The outer layer of paint.

Transom
A horizontal dividing member of a window frame.

Tread
The horizontal part of a step.

Undercoat
A layer of paint used to obliterate the colour of a primer and to build a protective body of paint prior to the application of a top coat.

Weatherboarding
Exterior wooden wall cladding.

Wood-boring insects
Beetles with larvae that feed on wood fibres. The most common variety is the furniture beetle or woodworm.